A Practical Guide to Drafting Pleadings

Fourmat Publishing

A Practical Guide to Drafting Pleadings
by Anthony Radevsky, Barrister

London
Fourmat Publishing
1991

ISBN 1 85190 141 8

First published 1991

Published by Fourmat Publishing
133 Upper Street Islington London N1 1QP

Printed in Great Britain by Billing & Sons Ltd, Worcester

To
Emily and Lucy

Foreword

by His Honour Judge Quentin Edwards QC

"It must be remembered that the accurate statement of such of the facts and circumstances of each case as are necessary to enable the plaintiff on the one hand to establish his entire cause of action and the defendant on the other to set up his entire defence is still an essential part of the duty of counsel".

Smith's Leading Cases, 4th edition (1856), page 103, edited by Willes and Keating JJ.

That wise comment was made upon the effect of the great reforms in practice and procedure of a hundred and fifty years ago. It is, to this day, an admirable epitome of what pleadings are. Counsel are not nowadays the only pleaders; many pleadings are drawn by solicitors but the duty, to court and client, is the same duty, resting on all lawyers, now as then.

The art of pleading is not valued sufficiently highly. Too often what is proffered to the court as pleadings looks like something knocked up in the shortest possible time by a draughtsman who has not thought about the case at all. This excellent manual on the elements and skills of pleading should be of much assistance to those who want to acquire and practise the art. For art it is; advocacy is generally held to be an art and pleading is a vital part of advocacy. Advocacy may be described as the fair presentation, in the most favourable light, of a litigant's case. The bones of that presentation are the pleading setting out the case, and if a party's case is not fully and carefully and accurately articulated in the pleading no later efforts, however beguiling, of the advocate will cure the defect or omission. I know the right to amend exists and is frequently exercised but how much more force there is in a case well and succinctly stated in the first instance. For, whether a pleading is subsequently amended or not, a mis-statement of a client's case can have a most serious effect upon his credit and the amendment of imprecise pleadings can lead to the waste of large sums in costs.

Some fundamental precepts must always be borne in mind. Statements, or particulars, of claim should state the plaintiff's case, not simply indicate that he has made, or is making, a claim; defences should likewise state the defence and not consist of a farrago of denials; delays should not be allowed, nor costs wasted, through requests for particulars which do not take the matter forward; discursive and elaborate language should always be eschewed. Simplicity and directness should be the goal, for a pleading is the distillation of a client's case. From the matrix of well-drawn pleadings a true compromise may be reached; if that desirable end cannot be attained the judge will, because the issues have been distinctly defined, be enabled to try the case in the shortest possible time, which is next in desirability to a compromise.

Mr. Anthony Radevsky has called his book *A Practical Guide to Drafting Pleadings*. Any lawyer undertaking litigation who gets his* hands on this book will find it to be straight forward, readable instruction on that very subject. If he puts that instruction into practice he will end as a sound pleader and, as an old hand in the law, I can say that is high praise for any practitioner in the courts of justice.

*Masculine is to be taken to include feminine!

Quentin Edwards
Bloomsbury County Court

Preface

This is a straightforward introductory guide to the drafting of pleadings. Regrettably, all too often, the importance of pleadings is not appreciated, and they are poorly drafted. The approach in this book is a practical one, concentrating on the rules of pleading, and the correct style to be adopted, with many worked examples. It is primarily intended to help the lawyer coming to pleadings afresh.

I wish to thank my colleagues in chambers for their helpful contributions. I am particularly grateful to Simon Brilliant for reading the first draft of the manuscript and making numerous improvements. Any errors are, of course, entirely my responsibility. I am also indebted to Liz Pickard and Montague Palfrey for their help with word-processing, and to my wife, Betty, for her patience and encouragement.

The law is up-to-date to 1 August 1991.

Publisher's Note

References to Order numbers throughout this book refer, unless specified otherwise, to the Rules of the Supreme Court 1965.

Contents

Chapter 1

An introduction to pleadings and formal requirements

1. What are pleadings?

In civil proceedings in England and Wales, the parties are under an obligation to serve on each other written documents setting out their respective cases. These documents are known as pleadings. The pleadings define the issues between the parties. A judge who has read the pleadings before the trial ought, if they have been well drafted, to know precisely which facts are agreed between the parties and which are in dispute.

The rules provide that "every pleading must contain, and contain only, a statement in a summary form of the material facts on which the party pleading relies for his claim or defence, as the case may be, but not the evidence by which those facts are to be proved, and the statement must be as brief as the nature of the case admits" (O 18 r 17(1)).

Three points arise immediately. First, in general, a pleading must contain facts only, and not legal arguments or evidence. Secondly, only material facts must be pleaded. Thirdly, the pleading must be as brief as possible.

Throughout this book, the rules will be explained with the use of worked examples. Later in this chapter, the first example is given, which considers these three points.

It should be noted that pleadings must not be confused with the originating process, ie the document by which proceedings are started. In the High Court, proceedings may be commenced by Writ of Summons, Originating Summons, Petition or Originating Motion. Pleadings are used only in actions started by Writ. Originating Summonses, Petitions and Originating Motions are outside the scope of this book.

1

The names of the pleadings are as follows:

In a High Court action begun by Writ —
the plaintiff starts by serving a **Statement of Claim**;
the defendant answers by serving a **Defence**;
the plaintiff may respond by serving a **Reply**.

If the defendant has a claim against the plaintiff, he may join a Counterclaim to his Defence. His pleading is then called a **Defence and Counterclaim**.

The Counterclaim is treated like a Statement of Claim, to which a Defence must be filed by the plaintiff. The plaintiff's pleading is called a **Reply and Defence to Counterclaim**.

Very occasionally, it may be necessary to serve a pleading subsequent to a Reply or a Defence to Counterclaim. The leave of the court is required to serve such a pleading (O 18 r 4), and this is dealt with in Chapter 9.

If a party's pleading is insufficiently clear or detailed, his opponent may serve a **Request for Further and Better Particulars** of the pleading, which must be answered.

In the county court, the names of the pleadings are the same except that the plaintiff's first pleading is called **Particulars of Claim**, not a Statement of Claim.

Example

We will start with the case of a man, knocked down and injured whilst crossing the road. He wishes to sue the driver of the car which hit him for damages for personal injury caused by the driver's negligence. Consider the following as the first paragraph of his Statement of Claim:

"In August 1990, the Plaintiff, a married man wearing a brown suit, was crossing Oxford Street in London to buy a shirt when the Defendant struck him with her car. The Defendant owed the Plaintiff a duty of care in negligence as a fellow road user. The accident was seen by a passer-by John Brown, who blamed the Defendant."

A number of the basic rules have been broken. First, three allegations are made which are not material to the claim; namely that the plaintiff was married, was wearing a brown suit and was going to buy a shirt. Secondly, the second

2

sentence is a proposition of law, and not a statement of fact. It is not necessary to allege in a traffic accident case that a duty of care was owed by one road user to another. The duty of care arises from the facts as pleaded. Thirdly, the last sentence is purely a matter of evidence. The witness, John Brown, may be called to give evidence at the trial, but what he saw, and who he blamed are not matters which may be pleaded.

Note also that the parties are called by their description, plaintiff or defendant, and not by their names. The details of time and place must be stated with precision, so that there cannot be any confusion as to which incident is being referred to.

A better attempt is as follows:

> "At about 3.30 p.m. on the 22nd August 1990, the Plaintiff was crossing Oxford Street, London W1 on foot from North to South at its junction with Wells Street, when a Ford Escort motor car registration no. G889 MGO being driven by the Defendant West along Oxford Street collided with the Plaintiff, and knocked him to the ground."

This paragraph sets the scene with precision. There can be no doubt as to which incident reference is being made. Thereafter, allegations of negligence will be dealt with.

2. Why pleadings are important

The importance of the pleadings in a case is often underestimated. This is a great mistake for several reasons. Because the pleadings define the issues between the parties, the judge is permitted to adjudicate only on the pleaded facts. However strong the evidence is in favour of one side, if it does not coincide with his pleadings, he cannot succeed. In order to do justice between the parties, the court has the power to allow any party to amend his pleadings at any stage. However, an amendment will almost always be allowed only on terms that the costs of the amendment (including the other side's costs of amending their pleading in reply, and the costs of any adjournment necessitated by the amendment) must be paid by the party wishing to amend.

The following are two good examples of the importance of pleadings:

3

(a) The decision of the Court of Appeal in *Fookes* v *Slaytor* [1978] 1 WLR 1293. The plaintiff, while driving at night, collided with an unlit trailer of a parked lorry. He sued the driver of the lorry in negligence. The driver did not serve a defence, and he was debarred from defending. The county court judge found that the defendant had been negligent, but found that the plaintiff had contributed to the accident by his own negligence and reduced his damages by one third. The Court of Appeal allowed the plaintiff's appeal, holding that contributory negligence had to be specifically pleaded by way of defence to a plaintiff's claim of negligence. Since there had been no such plea, the judge had erred in law in finding that the plaintiff's negligence had contributed to the accident.

(b) The decision of the House of Lords in *Esso Petroleum Co Ltd* v *Southport Corporation* [1956] AC 218. The plaintiff council sued the owners of an oil tanker which had run aground. To save the vessel, the ship's master had then discharged oil, which became deposited on the council's foreshore and caused damage. The plaintiff failed to prove the only negligence it pleaded, namely negligent navigation by the master. The plaintiff council contended that the vessel was not seaworthy at the start of the voyage. However, it had pleaded no allegation of unseaworthiness, and so could not succeed on this ground.

Since the pleadings define the issues between the parties, they also define the scope of interlocutory orders. After "close of pleadings", ie when the parties have finished serving their pleadings on each other, **discovery** usually takes place. This requires the parties to exchange lists of those documents relevant to the proceedings which they have (or had) in their possession. If there is a dispute as to relevance, it is to the pleadings that one must turn for the answer. Similarly, a party may serve **interrogatories** on the other seeking the answers to questions relevant to any matter in issue between them. Again, the pleadings are conclusive as to relevance.

The pleadings also determine much of the course of the trial. They show which party has the right to open the case, and upon whom the burden of proof lies on any particular issue.

As with interlocutory orders, it is the pleadings which determine relevance if a question as to the admissibility of evidence arises. The court is not entitled to grant a party specific relief which is not pleaded. If a party's evidence at trial differs from his pleaded case, the other side may rely on the discrepancy as bolstering their case. They may cross-examine the party as to why his evidence is different, since it will generally be assumed that the lawyer who drafted the pleading acted on his client's instructions! They may also comment strongly on any inconsistency at the end of the hearing. Judges not infrequently decide difficult conflicts of oral evidence by reference to consistency with documentary evidence.

If, after a trial, an allegation of *res judicata* is raised in the later proceedings, the pleadings in the first case provide the record of what was in issue for the purposes of that allegation.

3. Formal requirements

Order 18 r 6 sets out the formal requirements for every pleading. It states that:

"(1) Every pleading in an action must bear on its face —

> (a) the year in which the writ in the action was issued and the letter and number of the action,
> (b) the title of the action,
> (c) the division of the High Court to which the action is assigned and the name of the judge (if any) to whom it is assigned,
> (d) the description of the pleading, and
> (e) the date on which it was served.

(2) Every pleading must, if necessary, be divided into paragraphs numbered consecutively, each allegation being so far as convenient contained in a separate paragraph.

(3) Dates, sums and other numbers must be expressed in a pleading in figures and not in words.

(4) Every pleading of a party must be indorsed —

> (a) where the party sues or defends in person, with his name and address;

5

    (b) in any other case, with the name or firm and business address of the solicitor by whom it was served and also (if the solicitor is the agent of another) the name or firm and business address of his principal.

(5) Every pleading of a party must be signed by counsel, if settled by him, and, if not, by the party's solicitor or by the party, if he sues or defends in person."

The conventional layout is as follows:

IN THE HIGH COURT OF JUSTICE   1990 R No. 1234

QUEEN'S BENCH DIVISION

PORTSMOUTH DISTRICT REGISTRY

Writ issued the 1st day of August 1990

BETWEEN   JOHN HENRY ROCKET   <u>Plaintiff</u>

                       and

        PLUMMET INVESTMENTS LIMITED   <u>Defendant</u>

STATEMENT OF CLAIM

1.

2.

3.

AND the Plaintiff claims:

1.

2.

                              DERRICK PEARS

Served the 1st day of October 1990 by Grabbit Hard & Co. of 1 Oxbridge Street, London W1, Solicitors for the Plaintiff.

Note the following:

- In the top left hand corner, the court in which the action is proceeding is given. Under the words "**IN THE HIGH COURT OF JUSTICE**" the Division of the High Court is set out, and under that the District Registry, unless the Writ was issued in London. If the Writ is issued in the Commercial Court or in the list of Official Referees Business, those words appear on the

6

next line. The following line contains the name of the judge to which the action is assigned in those rare categories of case where there is such an assignment.

- In the case of a Statement of Claim, the date the Writ was issued should be given on the following line. However, this does not apply to a Statement of Claim which is indorsed on the Writ.

- The number of the action is set out in the top right hand corner. The first number is the year when the Writ is issued. Then comes the letter of the action. In the case of an individual as plaintiff (or first plaintiff) it is the first letter of his surname. If the plaintiff (or first plaintiff) is a limited company or other non-personal entity, the letter is the first letter of its name (omitting "The"). The last number is allocated by the court when the Writ is issued.

- The names of the parties must be set out in full, if known. In Appendix A, a table of the correct form of parties is set out. All the names of an individual should be given, if possible. The word "Limited" should be set out in full, not "Ltd". In the case of more than one plaintiff or defendant, the better practice is to number and name them on separate lines, as follows:

(1) WILLIAM SHAKESPEARE
(2) THESPIAN BUILDERS LIMITED   <u>Defendants</u>

- Where a party is suing or is sued in a representative capacity, that capacity is stated in the title. In the Chancery Division it is mentioned in the body of the pleading.

- The description of the pleading is then given, eg **STATEMENT OF CLAIM**. Where the pleading is in two parts, eg **DEFENCE AND COUNTERCLAIM**, the full description is given first, followed by DEFENCE on the next line. The word COUNTER-CLAIM is inserted immediately following the body of the Defence.

- After the description comes the text of the party's pleading, known as the body of the pleading. This must be divided into paragraphs consecutively. A common error is to start numbering again in the case of a Counterclaim. However, since the **DEFENCE AND COUNTERCLAIM** is treated as a single pleading, the numbering follows on from the Defence.

- So far as possible, each allegation must be contained in a separate paragraph. Not only is this laid down in the rules, but it is also of practical help in ensuring that the facts are clearly presented. The first pleading, being the Statement of Claim, should be drafted with this rule particularly in mind. It makes the drafting of the Defence easier, by enabling each allegation to be dealt with in turn. It is also helpful to plead the Statement of Claim in strict chronological order. This will be dealt with in more detail later.

- All numbers, including dates and sums of money must be expressed in figures and not in words. It is wrong, therefore, to plead a sum of money as "£150 (one hundred and fifty pounds)". Just the figures will do.

- The pleading must be signed by the draftsman. In practice, where counsel settles the pleading, he signs the draft which is sent to the solicitor. The solicitor engrosses the pleading for service, and counsel's name is typed on to the bottom; this is perfectly acceptable. Counsel's name should not be omitted from a pleading, nor should counsel's name be included when he has not settled the pleading! Where the pleading is drafted by a solicitor, the signature of his clerk is sufficient.

- In the Statement of Claim, the relief sought is set out after the body of the pleading in the prayer, which states "AND the Plaintiff claims ...", followed by numbered paragraphs setting out the relief, eg damages, an injunction, interest. The method of pleading the prayer is dealt with in more detail in Chapter 5.

RSC Order 66 sets out the requirements as to paper, printing, provision of copies etc in respect of all documents for use in the Supreme Court, including pleadings:

Paper

Pleadings must be prepared on A4 paper of durable quality.

Layout

A blank 1½ inch margin must be left on the left side of the face of the paper, and on the right side of the reverse.

Writing

Every pleading must be:

(a) printed (including production by type lithography or stencil duplicating),
(b) written clearly and legibly, or
(c) typewritten (otherwise than by means of a carbon).

It may contain a mixture of the permissible methods. A clear photocopy of one of the permissible methods is as good as the original.

Size of type

Any type used must be clear and legible and not smaller than 11 point type for printing or elite type for type lithography, stencil duplicating or typewriting.

Copies

If a pleading is printed and another party entitled to a copy requests in writing up to ten copies, those copies must be supplied upon payment of the proper charges.

If the pleading is written or typewritten, any other party who is entitled to a copy (not being a party on whom it has been served) must be supplied with one copy on request, within 48 hours of the request, provided the proper charges are paid.

Chapter 2

The style of drafting

At first glance a layman might regard many pleadings as being verbose and full of archaic and legalistic language. It is undoubtedly true that some pleadings leave much to be desired from the point of view of clarity. Although the style of pleading is in many ways a very personal matter, it is suggested that the following principles should be followed.

1. Use of English

Pleadings must be written in clear grammatical English. Slang or colloquial expressions must never be used. Although using a split infinitive or ending a sentence with a preposition will obviously not invalidate a pleading, it may irritate certain judges.

When you have finished drafting any pleading, check it carefully to make sure that it reads properly. It should be unambiguous and correctly punctuated. Although many leases avoid punctuation altogether, this style should not be copied in the drafting of pleadings in order to make them sound more legal! It is as well to have in mind that one day, perhaps years later, three judges in the Court of Appeal might be scrutinising a particular word or sentence in order to rule on whether the client's case is properly pleaded (for an example where one word of the author's own pleading was thus analysed, see *Longman* v *Viscount Chelsea* [1989] 2 EGLR 242 at page 246F).

2. Cause of action

When drafting a Statement of Claim, make sure it discloses a cause of action. It may be helpful to read it through, pretending you are on the other side trying to challenge the claim made. It will be necessary to have in mind the essential elements of the cause of action that is being relied upon.

For example, a cause of action in negligence requires three elements:

    (a) a duty of care owed to the plaintiff by the defendant;
    (b) a breach of that duty of care;
    (c) damage flowing from the breach.

Have the facts giving rise to all three been pleaded?

3. Be concise

This is not only a requirement of the rules (O 18 r 7(1)), but it is also a matter of good style. If you can use two words to say what you mean, do not use four.

For example, when giving particulars of the defendant's negligence in a road traffic accident claim, plead only those which are actually relevant to the claim. The defendant might have caused the accident simply by not looking where he was going. If so, do not add a makeweight allegation that he was driving too fast in all the circumstances, if there is no evidence to suggest that he was.

4. Be precise

In some ways this is the most important single rule. It is also the one which leads to the problem of complicated and archaic language. Because of the need to avoid any possibility of ambiguity, it is customary to ensure that repeated references to the same thing are identified.

For example, in a claim for possession of a house, the first reference to the property in the pleading will specify the address and extent of the property claimed. It will be necessary to refer to the house on a number of subsequent occasions in the pleading. Rather than repeat the address each time, the property can be referred to as "the said premises". Alternatively, after the first reference to the property, one can use the phrase "hereinafter called 'the premises'". Some people go further and shorten this by omitting the words "hereinafter called".

Thus:

1. The Plaintiff is the freehold owner of the premises comprising a house and garden, known as 1 Acacia Gardens, London SW1, hereinafter called "the premises".

2. By a tenancy agreement dated the 1st January 1990, the Plaintiff let the premises to the Defendant for 1 year at a rent of £100 per month.

Or:

1. The Plaintiff is the freehold owner of the premises comprising a house and garden, known as 1 Acacia Gardens, London SW1.

2. By a tenancy agreement dated the 1st January 1990, the Plaintiff let the said premises to the Defendant for 1 year at a rent of £100 per month.

Note the use of the word "hereinafter". Although it is archaic, it is useful because it avoids the use of a longer phrase such as "which will be called on future occasions in the Statement of Claim". Other similar old-fashioned words which are commonly used to shorten pleadings are "hereinbelow", "hereinabove", "heretofore". Overuse of these words should be avoided.

The reason why such precision is necessary is to avoid any possible ambiguity. In the above example, it is necessary to be sure at each stage which premises are being referred to. It may be that there is an allegation of nuisance from neighbouring premises; the judge reading the pleadings must not be confused as to which premises reference is being made.

One not uncommon error is to do a "belt and braces" job and plead after the address — "hereinafter called 'the said premises'".

Whilst discussing the description of "premises", it is appropriate to mention one common expression which can be confusing for the beginner. When pleading a conclusion which follows from earlier paragraphs in a pleading, the words "In the premises ..." are often used, meaning "In view of what has gone before ...". When drafting pleadings in proceedings relating to land, it is necessary to take care not to confuse that expression with "premises" meaning land or property.

5. Be consistent

Following on the requirement for precision, it is also important that consistency is maintained when referring to the same person or thing. Thus, if reference is once made to "the premises", do not then refer to "the said premises", or "the said flat" or "Flat 1, 30 Acacia Road", but keep referring to "the premises".

6. Dates and places

Most pleadings include one or more dates. In pleading an accident, it is usual to refer to both the date and time of day when it occurred. It is easy to make a slip as to the date, and to get it wrong by one day. If the evidence shows that the pleaded date is wrong, it will be necessary to make a formal amendment to the pleading. Consequently, in order to avoid that possibility, dates are often preceded by the words "On or about" or "In or about", thus:

1. On or about the 14th May 1990, the Plaintiff . . .

   or:

2. In or about October 1977, the Defendant purchased . . .

Similarly, times are usually preceded by "At about", thus:

1. At about 11.30 a.m. on or about the 1st March 1991 . . .

There is no need to write the date out in full (as in some legal documents) as in "the 22nd day of May 1990". The 22nd May 1990 will do.

Addresses

Land and premises are given their full address (though not the postcode). It used to be thought incorrect to refer to the county by its ordinary name (eg Warwickshire), but correct to say "in the County of Warwick", specifying the county town. Thus, instead of Hampshire, one would have said "in the County of Southampton". The reorganisation of local government and the modernisation of language have rendered this practice obsolete.

7. Material facts

The introductory chapter mentioned the fundamental content of pleadings, namely that they comprise the material facts on which a party relies, set out as briefly as possible. It is necessary now to examine this idea in more detail.

(a) Facts, not evidence, must be pleaded

It is not always easy to distinguish between facts and evidence, but, for instance, an allegation that an incident was witnessed by someone should not be pleaded, nor should an admission made by another party, since both are matters of evidence.

This rule is subject to the exceptions contained in O 18 r 7A.

(i) Conviction of an offence (s 11 Civil Evidence Act 1968)

By r 7A(1), if a party intends to adduce evidence that a person was convicted of an offence (by or before a court in the United Kingdom or by a court-martial there or elsewhere) he must include in his pleading:

(a) a statement of his intention; and
(b) particulars of:

- the conviction and the date thereof,
- the court or court-martial which made the conviction, and
- the issue in the proceedings to which the conviction is relevant.

This rule does not apply to foreign convictions, which must not be pleaded. Typically, a conviction will be relied upon in a claim for damages for personal injury following a road traffic accident for which the defendant has been convicted of, say, driving without due care and attention. The conviction, to the criminal standard of proof, is compelling evidence of negligence.

Example

The Plaintiff intends to rely upon the Defendant's conviction for driving without due care and attention at Wimbledon Magistrates' Court on the 14th March 1991, arising from the matters pleaded above, as evidence of his negligence.

14

(ii) Adultery or paternity (s 12 Civil Evidence Act 1968)

By r 7A(2), if a party intends to adduce evidence that a person was found guilty of adultery in matrimonial proceedings or has been found to be the father of a child in relevant proceedings before any court in England and Wales or has been adjudged to be the father of a child in affiliation proceedings before a court in the United Kingdom, he must include in his pleading:

(a) a statement of his intention; and
(b) particulars of:

- the finding or adjudication and the date thereof,
- the court which made the finding or adjudication and the proceedings in which it was made, and
- the issue in the proceedings to which the finding or adjudication is relevant.

(iii) Challenging a conviction etc

If the opposite party facing a pleaded allegation of a conviction, adultery or paternity:

(a) denies the conviction, finding or adjudication of paternity to which the statement relates; or
(b) alleges that the conviction, finding or adjudication was erroneous; or
(c) denies that the conviction, finding or adjudication is relevant to any issue in the proceedings,

he must make the denial or allegation in his pleading.

Note that, by virtue of s 13 Civil Evidence Act 1968, a conviction may not be challenged in a defamation action.

The pleading must specify precisely in which way the challenge is being made; a general denial is not good enough, not least because it does not specify under which ground the challenge is being made.

The onus is on the party attempting to disprove the conviction or finding of adultery. If it is alleged that a conviction is erroneous or that an admitted conviction is irrelevant to the civil proceedings, this is setting up a positive case requiring particulars to be given.

(b) Facts, not law, must be pleaded

This rule of practice means that, whereas the facts giving rise to legal conclusions are to be pleaded, the legal conclusions themselves should not be pleaded, and nor should general statements of law.

Example

The plaintiff was injured in a road traffic accident by a lorry driven by an employee of the company which owned the lorry. The driver was doing his work when the accident took place. The plaintiff wishes to sue the company but not the driver (who has no money), the company being liable by virtue of the principle of vicarious liability. The following is correct:

> On the 1st May 1992, at about 10 p.m. the Plaintiff was crossing Goldhawk Road, Leeds, Yorkshire by the pedestrian crossing next to the Hornet Building Society, when a Magirus Deutz lorry registration no. F564 GJN owned by the Defendant and driven by its employee, Brian Slagg, who was acting in the course of his employment, collided with the Plaintiff.

It is incorrect to add, "An employer is vicariously liable for the negligence of its employees whilst acting in the course of their employment." That is a matter of legal principle which the court will consider if and when the pleaded material facts are proved at the hearing.

Even worse is to refer to reported cases as authority for propositions of law.

(c) A point of law may be pleaded

In contrast to the previous rule, a party may by his pleading raise any point of law (O 18 r 11).

This rule is concerned with the raising of a matter of law on the facts as pleaded, which may well lead to the trial of a preliminary issue to decide the point of law.

For example, a party may allege that, as a matter of law, the construction of the contract contended for by the other side is unsustainable, or that damages are not recoverable on the basis of the facts pleaded because no duty of care arises.

(d) Documents and conversations

It is often necessary to refer to documents or conversations in pleadings, for instance to establish the existence of a contract. By O 18 r 7(2), the *effect* of any document or the *purport* of any conversation referred to in a pleading must, if material, be briefly stated, and the precise words of the documents or conversation should not be stated, except in so far as those words are themselves material.

The purpose of this rule is to avoid pleadings becoming excessively lengthy. Regrettably, the rule is sometimes not followed, and a pleading sets out verbatim numerous clauses in a contract or lease where the actual words are not important to the case.

Example

The claim is for forfeiture of a lease for non-payment of rent. The forfeiture clause (which must, of course, be pleaded) is twenty-five lines long and provides for a right of re-entry in the event of a long list of occurrences (breach of covenant, bankruptcy etc) with which this claim is not concerned. Rather than repeat the whole clause, all that is needed is a relatively short paraphrase:

> 5. Clause 5 of the lease contained a right of re-entry in the event that the said rent was 21 days in arrears.

(e) Presumptions

By O 18 r 7(3), a party need not plead any fact (i) if it is presumed by law to be true or (ii) the burden of disproving it lies on the other party, unless the other party has specifically denied it in his pleading.

(f) Condition precedent

> "A statement that a thing has been done or that an event has occurred, being a thing or event the doing or occurrence of which, as the case may be, constitutes a condition precedent necessary for the case of a party is to be implied in his pleading" (O 18 r 7(4)).

This rule removes the requirement to plead a condition

precedent which falls short of one of the material facts forming part of the cause of action or defence.

For example, it is a condition precedent to the bringing of a claim for forfeiture of a lease (other than for non-payment of rent) that a notice under s 146 Law of Property Act 1925 has been served on the lessee and has not been complied with. Although the notice is generally pleaded, it has been held unnecessary to do so, by virtue of this rule.

(g) Alternative allegations

Within a single pleading, a party may make alternative allegations which are inconsistent with each other. For instance, a plaintiff landowner may allege (i) that the defendant has always been a trespasser on the land, alternatively (ii) that the defendant was a licensee of the land and that his licence has been determined by reasonable notice served without prejudice to (i), alternatively that the defendant was a tenant of the land and that the tenancy has been determined by a notice to quit served without prejudice to (i) and (ii).

However, a party's primary contention must be made clear, and any alternatives must be pleaded to make it plain how the case is put. Thus, in the example above, the relevant paragraphs of the pleading might read as follows:

1. The Plaintiff is the freehold owner and entitled to possession of the premises known as 54 Grange Road, Eltham, Kent.

2. In or about March 1987, the Defendant entered the said premises and has remained in occupation ever since without the consent of the Plaintiff.

3. Alternatively, if which is denied, the Defendant was the licensee of the Plaintiff in the said premises, such licence was determined by a letter written on the 14th March 1991 by the Plaintiff's Solicitor, without prejudice to the contention that the Defendant was a trespasser. The licence was determined on the 30th June 1991, but the Defendant has remained in unlawful occupation of the said premises.

4. In the further alternative, if which is denied, the Defendant was a tenant of the said premises, his tenancy was determined was a Notice to Quit, served on the 14th March 1991 without prejudice to the contention that the Defendant was a trespasser, terminating the tenancy on the 18th April 1991. The Defendant's tenancy (which is denied) was at no rent and is, in the premises, not protected by the Rent Act 1977.

(h) Departure

What a party may not do, however, is to allege any fact or raise any new ground or claim which is inconsistent with a previous pleading (O 18 r 10(1)). Thus, if the claim in the Statement of Claim is that the defendant is a trespasser, and the defence pleads that the defendant is a tenant, the plaintiff cannot in his Reply claim rent from the defendant as tenant. The appropriate course of action is to amend the Statement of Claim to plead the claim for rent in the alternative. This is specifically provided for in O 18 r 10(2), which states that r 10 (1) "shall not be taken as prejudicing the right of a party to amend, or apply for leave to amend, his previous pleading so as to plead the allegations or claims in the alternative".

(i) Time when matters pleaded arose

The general rule is that any matter may be pleaded which has arisen at any time, whether before or since the issue of the Writ (O 18 r 9). This rule is expressed to be subject to three other rules:

  (i) Order 18 r 7(1), the general rule as to the content of pleadings, namely that they must contain material facts, and not evidence.
 (ii) Order 18 r 10, the rule precluding departure from a previous pleading (see *(h)* above).
(iii) Order 18 r 15(2), limiting the contents of the Statement of Claim.

It is this rule, combined with O 18 r 15(2), which creates a potential difficulty with claims that overlap the date of issue of the Writ.

Example

A contract provides for the price to be paid by ten instalments. The defendant defaults on two, and the plaintiff issues a Writ. By the time of the hearing, no other instalments have been paid. Can the plaintiff claim the further instalments in the existing proceedings, or must he start fresh proceedings?

Order 18 r 15(2) provides that a Statement of Claim must not contain any allegation or claim in respect of a cause of action unless that cause of action is mentioned in the Writ or arises from facts which are the same as, or include or form part of, facts giving rise to a cause of action so mentioned; but, subject to that, a plaintiff may in his Statement of Claim alter, modify or extend any claim made by him in the indorsement of the Writ without amending the indorsement.

Going back to the example, the question arises if and when the plaintiff seeks to amend the Statement of Claim to include the later instalments. Two conflicting High Court decisions give different answers. In *Zea Star Shipping* v *Parley Augustsson* [1984] 2 Lloyd's Rep 605, Sheen J granted the plaintiff leave to amend the claim to include non-payment of instalments due after the issue of the writ, holding that there was nothing in the Rules of the Supreme Court to prevent such an amendment. However, that decision was not followed by Neill J in *The C and J* [1984] 2 Lloyd's Rep 601. On indistinguishable facts, the court held that the universal practice was not to grant leave to amend the pleadings to include causes of action arising after the issue of the Writ. It is generally accepted that the latter of two conflicting first instance decisions should be preferred, particularly when it refers to the former, as here.

Accordingly, the correct practice should be assumed to be that one has to bring a fresh set of proceedings to claim sums falling due after the Writ is issued. What is sometimes done is to issue another Writ, and ask that both sets of proceedings be consolidated and heard at the same time. If time is short, leave can be given to dispense with some of the formalities of the second action.

Forfeiture of lease: An effective exception to the general practice exists in the case of forfeiture of a lease. Forfeiture is effected by service of the Writ, not by its issue (*Canas Property Co Ltd* v *KL Television Services Ltd* [1970] 2 QB 433), and so rent should be claimed up to the date of service of the Writ, and mesne profits (ie compensation for use and occupation) thereafter.

Continuing claims: In contrast to the payment of a contract price by instalments, when each non-payment founds a new cause of action, in some cases a single claim arises from a continuous course of acting.

Examples

(i) In a claim for nuisance by noise from a neighbour, which is continuing, the court will be able to award damages for the period after the proceedings have been issued.

(ii) In an action for possession, the plaintiff claims mesne profits from the date of service of proceedings until the defendant delivers up possession.

It is not always easy to draw the dividing line between these two types of claim.

Chapter 3

The ethics of pleading

In a lecture given to young barristers in the Middle Temple in 1964, Salmon LJ said:

> "You will sometimes be instructed to make an allegation of fraud. You must never sign any pleading making such an allegation unless you have been placed in possession of material which appears reliable and which if accepted by the court would establish a prima facie case of fraud. It may happen that a client may ask you to allege fraud on flimsy material or even on no material at all. You must refuse such a request however much your refusal may displease your client. When an allegation of fraud is made the other side may pay up if they are defendants or throw in their hand if they are plaintiffs rather than risk the publicity of facing such an allegation in court, unfounded though it may be. To make such an allegation of fraud therefore without proper material is an abuse of the process of the court and a potent form of blackmail. I need hardly tell you that the traditions of the Bar will not permit counsel to be party to blackmail."

The draftsman of pleadings has the benefit of absolute privilege to protect him or her from an action in defamation. Although the court may strike out scandalous, frivolous or vexatious allegations in pleadings (under O 18 r 19), further protection from abuse is laid down in professional rules.

1. Barristers

For barristers, the ethical principles of pleading are set out in paragraph 606 of the current *Code of Conduct of the Bar of*

22

England and Wales (effective from 31 March 1990). This states:

"A practising barrister must not devise facts which will assist in advancing his lay client's case and must not draft any originating process, pleading, affidavit, witness statement or notice of appeal containing:

(a) any statement of fact or contention (as the case may be) which is not supported by his lay client or by his brief or instructions;
(b) any contention which he does not consider to be properly arguable;
(c) any allegation of fraud unless he has clear instructions to make such allegation and has before him reasonably credible material which as it stands establishes a prima facie case of fraud;
(d) in the case of an affidavit or witness statement any statement of fact other than the evidence which in substance according to his instructions the barrister reasonably believes the witness would give if the evidence contained in the affidavit or witness statement were being given *viva voce;*

Provided that nothing in this paragraph shall prevent a barrister drafting a pleading, affidavit or witness statement containing specific facts matters or contentions included by the barrister subject to the lay client's confirmation as to their accuracy."

This rule recognises the dilemma in which a barrister is sometimes placed by his lay client and/or instructing solicitor. It is often difficult in practice to resolve the dilemma, and guidance may be sought from more senior colleagues or the Professional Conduct Committee of the Bar.

The following notes may assist:

- In the case of an ordinary factual allegation, this must be supported either by his written or oral instructions from the solicitor or lay client. If the barrister is in any doubt, he should ask for specific written instructions on the particular matter, signed by the client or witness, as appropriate.
- Where the barrister is asked to plead a contention that is not properly arguable, he must not do so. What is

meant by properly arguable? It is the author's view that any contention may be made which is not bound to fail. However, if the point is a weak one, this should always be pointed out to the client in a separate note or advice.

- Allegations of fraud are particularly sensitive, and paragraph 606(c) of the *Code of Conduct* reflects Salmon LJ's strictures. It is normally necessary to have some corroborative evidence of fraud before pleading it, such as more than one signed witness statement and/or documentary evidence.

- The proviso to paragraph 606 permits the barrister to include in the draft pleading a request that the accuracy of a particular allegation be specifically confirmed by the client. However, it is usually better to obtain the confirmation first, and send out a complete draft. Otherwise, if the client does not provide the necessary confirmation, or there remains some doubt, the papers will have to be returned to the barrister for re-drafting.

2. Solicitors

The Law Society's *Guide to the Professional Conduct of Solicitors* (1990) makes no express reference to pleadings. However, Chapter 14 of the Guide deals with the relationship between the solicitor and the court.

Paragraph 14.01 states that "A solicitor who acts in litigation, whilst owing a duty to his client to do his best for him, must never deceive or mislead the court."

It is considered that a solicitor drafting pleadings or other documents, who fails to observe the Bar's rules set out above, runs the risk of deceiving or misleading the court.

3. Sanctions

Apart from amounting to professional misconduct, pleading an unarguable claim amounts to an abuse of process, and sometimes even to a contempt of court!

A cautionary tale is told in the case of *R* v *Weisz ex parte Hector MacDonald Ltd* [1951] 2 KB 611. A solicitor was instructed by his client to bring an action against bookmakers for money alleged to be owed by them to the client on bets. The client insisted that the action be brought, even though he knew that it was not maintainable in law, in the hope that the threat of publicity would induce the bookmakers to pay up, or, if they did not, for the purpose of "showing them up". A specially indorsed Writ was issued against the bookmakers by which the money was claimed to be due on an account stated. However, no account had been stated, as the solicitor knew. The client did not know of the terms of the indorsement. The Divisional Court held that the solicitor had committed a contempt of court because the indorsement on the Writ was fictitious and was designed to conceal from the court the true nature of the claim. The solicitor apologised, and as the court found no intention to act in contempt, no penalty was imposed.

Chapter 4

Indorsement on Writ

Chapter 5 deals with the drafting of a Statement of Claim. When a Writ is issued, it may be indorsed with a Statement of Claim, in which case it is usually known as a "specially indorsed Writ". However, a plaintiff sometimes wishes to issue a Writ without pleading a full Statement of Claim, perhaps because there is no time to draft one, or the full facts which need to be pleaded have not yet been assembled. In those cases he may do so, provided it is indorsed "with a concise statement of the nature of the claim made or the relief or remedy required in the action begun thereby": O 6 r 2(1)(a). This document is usually called a "generally indorsed Writ". This procedure is used, for example, when:

(i) it is necessary to issue a Writ shortly before the expiry of the limitation period; or

(ii) an interlocutory order (eg a *Mareva* injunction) is sought speedily at the outset of proceedings which must be launched by a Writ.

The indorsement begins "The Plaintiff's claim is for . . . " and these words are printed on the top of the obverse side of the Writ form.

If a Statement of Claim is not indorsed on the Writ, the indorsement of the concise statement of the nature of the claim is not a pleading, but is nevertheless dealt with in this book. Examples are given below. Order 6 r 2 states what must be indorsed on the Writ in addition to the Statement of Claim or "concise statement of the nature of the claim made" etc. These requirements may (if appropriate) be included in the Statement of Claim if one is indorsed on the Writ.

26

1. Debt claims

Where the claim made by the plaintiff is for a debt or liquidated demand *only*, the Writ must be indorsed with a statement of the amount claimed in respect of the debt or demand and for costs and also with a statement that further proceedings will be stayed if, within the time limited for acknowledging service, the defendant pays the amount so claimed to the plaintiff, his solicitor or agent (O 6 r 2(1)(b)).

Example

After the concise statement of the nature of the claim −

If, within the time for returning the Acknowledgement of Service, the Defendant pays the amount claimed and £ [insert appropriate figure contained in RSC O 62, Appendix 3] for costs and, if the Plaintiff obtains an order for substituted service, the additional sum of £ [insert], further proceedings will be stayed. The money must be paid to the Plaintiff, his Solicitor or agent.

"Liquidated demand" is a claim which is in the nature of a debt in that it is a specific sum of money due under a contract. Its amount must either already have been calculated, or be capable of being immediately calculated by simple arithmetic. If any further investigation is required to determine the amount, the sum claimed is properly described as "damages". A claim for genuine liquidated damages (as opposed to a penalty) is a liquidated demand, as is a claim for reasonable remuneration (quantum meruit).

(a) Foreign currency

(i) For the purpose of ascertaining the proper amount of the costs to be indorsed on the Writ, where the plaintiff makes a claim for a debt or liquidated demand expressed in a foreign currency, the Writ must be indorsed with the following certificate, which must be signed by or on behalf of the solicitor of the plaintiff or by the plaintiff if he is acting in person:

Sterling equivalent of amount claimed
I/We certify that the rate current in London for the purchase of (state the unit of the foreign currency claimed) at the close of business on the [insert date next to or most nearly preceding the date of the issue of the Writ] was [insert] to the £ sterling and at this rate the debt or

liquidated demand claimed herein, namely [state the sum of the foreign currency claimed] amounts to [insert] or exceeds £3,000 [as the case may be].
Dated the . . . day of . . . 19..

Signed . . . .

(Solicitor for the Plaintiff)

(ii) Where the plaintiff seeks to obtain a judgment expressed in a foreign currency, he should expressly state in his Writ of Summons, *whether indorsed with a Statement of Claim or not*, that he makes his claim for payment in a specified foreign currency and, unless the facts themselves clearly show this, he should plead the facts relied on to support such a claim in his Statement of Claim (*Queen's Bench Masters' Practice Direction 11*).

(b) Interest

Claims for interest are not expressly referred to in O 6 r 2. However, the reference to a debt or liquidated demand includes a claim for interest, by virtue of O 13 r 1(2) which deals with the entry of judgment in default of a notice of intention to defend having been given. Consequently, although a claim for interest on a debt or liquidated demand need not be set out in a generally indorsed Writ, it is desirable that it is.

By O 18 r 8(4), any claim for interest, whether under s 35A Supreme Court Act 1981 or otherwise, must be specifically pleaded.

The claim for interest should be pleaded in the body of the Statement of Claim, as well as in the prayer. It must set out both the basis of the claim and, where interest is claimed on a sum of money and can be calculated, the amount claimed. There are a number of different bases for the claim: for example, under the terms of a contract between the parties, under s 35A Supreme Court Act 1981, or under other statutes such as the Bills of Exchange Act 1882.

The pleading requirements for claims for interest on debts or liquidated sums are set out in *Practice Note (Claims for Interest) (No. 2)* [1983] 1 WLR 377:

(i) Interest under s 35A Supreme Court Act 1981

Indorsements complying with O 13 r 1(2): The procedure where a debt or liquidated demand is claimed is the same as for claims for contractual interest, for which see paragraph (ii) below. [NB When judgment in default of giving notice of intention to defend is entered, O 13 r 1(2) provides that a claim is not prevented from being treated as a liquidated demand merely because interest under s 35A is claimed.]

(a) The Statement of Claim must plead:

- the cause of action, with particulars, the sum claimed and the date when payment was due;
- the claim for interest under s 35A Supreme Court Act 1981, the rate of interest claimed and the amount of interest claimed from the date when payment was due to the date of issue of the Writ.

   (The rate of interest claimed must not exceed the rate of interest on judgment debts current at the date of issue of the Writ. The current rate is 15%, and has been so since 1985.)

(b) The Statement of Claim should also include a claim for further interest at the aforesaid rate under the Act from the date of issue of Writ to judgment or sooner payment. This should be shown as a daily rate to assist calculation when judgment is entered.

(c) See paragraph (ii)(b) below for the 14-day costs indorsement.

   Indorsements for interest to be assessed: If the plaintiff seeks interest at a higher rate than current judgment debts interest, or for any other reason requires interest on a debt to be assessed, he must plead a claim for interest under s 35A Supreme Court Act 1981 and enter judgment for interest to be assessed.

(ii) Contractual interest

(a) The Statement of Claim must give sufficient particulars of the contract relied on, and, in particular, must show:

- the date from which interest is payable;
- the rate of interest fixed by the contract;

- the amount of interest due at the issue of the Writ.

(b) The interest up to the issue of the Writ should be claimed in the prayer and included in the sum entered in the indorsement for 14-day costs. This indorsement must be made; if the defendant pays the principal sum, the interest to the date of the Writ and the 14-day costs within the 14 days, the action is stayed and no further interest is payable.

(c) The Statement of Claim should also contain a prayer for further interest at the contract rate from the issue of the Writ to judgment or sooner payment. It is often helpful to work out and show this interest also as a daily rate.

(d) If the defendant makes default in giving notice of intention to defend or in serving a Defence, the plaintiff may sign judgment for the principal sum, interest to the date of the Writ, further interest calculated to the date of the judgment and scale costs. This last calculation is checked by the court when judgment is entered, and it is for this reason that the Statement of Claim must give sufficient information to enable this to be done quickly.

(iii) Interest under the Bills of Exchange Act 1882

(a) By s 57 of this Act the holder of a cheque (or other bill of exchange) which is dishonoured when duly presented is entitled to recover, in addition to the amount of the cheque, interest as liquidated damages from the date of dishonour until the date of judgment or sooner payment.

(b) There is no prescribed rate of interest; the plaintiff may properly ask for a reasonable rate around or somewhat above base rate. If a high rate is asked, there may be difficulty in entering a default judgment while the matter is referred to the practice master (s 57(3) of the Act). Short-term investment account rate is a safe guide.

(c) The Statement of Claim should set out the date of dishonour, the rate of interest claimed, a calculation of the interest due at the date of the issue of the Writ, and prayers for this interest and further interest until judgment or sooner payment. The procedure is as explained for contractual interest in paragraphs (ii)(b) to (d) above.

Note: – the expression "judgment or sooner payment" is used in this note because the right to interest after the judgment is almost always under the Judgments Act *only*.

Unliquidated claims: The claim for interest in an indorsement on a Writ is usually given as "... and interest pursuant to Section 35A of the Supreme Court Act 1981."

In a Statement of Claim, the claim for interest in the body of the pleading will read as follows:

> 10. Further, the Plaintiff is entitled to and claims interest on such damages as he is awarded, pursuant to Section 35A of the Supreme Court Act 1981 at such rate and for such period as this Honourable Court thinks fit.

Then in the prayer, the claim can refer back to the Statement of Claim, thus:

> AND the Plaintiff claims:
> 1. Damages;
> 2. Interest therein under paragraph 10 hereof, to be assessed.

With regard to interest in personal injury claims, interest on special damages between the accident and trial is generally awarded at half the normal rate provided by s 35A Supreme Court Act 1981 (currently 15%). However, there may be exceptional cases where the court will award interest at the full rate. If the plaintiff wishes to argue for the full rate, he must plead the facts relied on in the claim for interest: *Dexter* v *Courtaulds Ltd* [1984] 1 WLR 372.

2. Possession of land

Order 6 r 2(1)(c) provides that where the claim made by the plaintiff is for possession of land, the Writ must be indorsed with a statement showing:

"(i) whether the claim relates to a dwelling-house; and

(ii) if it does, whether the rateable value of the premises on every day specified by section 4(2) of the Rent Act 1977 in relation to the premises exceeds the sum so specified, or whether the rent for the time being payable in respect of the premises exceeds the sum specified in section 4(4)(b) of the Rent Act 1977; and

(iii) in a case where the plaintiff knows of any person entitled to claim relief against forfeiture as underlessee (including a mortgagee) under section 146(4) of the Law of Property Act 1925 or in accordance with section 38 of the Supreme Court Act 1981, the name and address of that person" (in such a case the plaintiff must send a copy of the Writ to the person named).

Section 4 Rent Act 1977 (dealing with the rateable value limits) was amended as a result of the abolition of domestic rates on 31 March 1990. For tenancies where the premises consequently have no rateable value on the appropriate day, the Rent Act cannot apply if the rent exceeds £25,000 per annum. *Queen's Bench Masters' Practice Direction 10* sets out suggested forms of indorsement for claims for possession of dwelling-houses containing the information in (i) and (ii):

As regards tenancies for which the appropriate day was before 1 April 1990:

The premises are a dwelling-house situate [in Greater London] [elsewhere than in Greater London] and the rateable value thereof was as follows:

(a) on the appropriate day (if before March 22, 1973) in excess of [£400][£200]

(b) on March 22, 1973 in excess of [£600][£300]

(c) on or after April 1, 1973 in excess of [£1,500][£750].

As regards tenancies for which the appropriate day was on or after 1 April 1990:

The premises are a dwelling-house the tenancy of which —

(i) was entered into on or after April 1, 1990; and

(ii) was not entered into pursuant to a contract made before April 1, 1990 with respect to premises which had a rateable value on March 31, 1990; and

(iii) provides for a rental payable for the time being at a rate exceeding £25,000 a year.

The claim "relates to a dwelling-house" even if only part of the premises is occupied as such. If it does not relate to a dwelling-house, for the avoidance of doubt, the Statement of Claim conventionally states: "No part of the premises comprises a dwelling-house."

3. Possession of goods

Where the action is brought to enforce a right to recover possession of goods, the Writ must be indorsed with a statement showing the value of the goods (O 6 r 2(1)(d)).

4. Consumer credit agreement

Where the action relates to a consumer credit agreement, the Writ must be indorsed with a certificate that the action is not one to which s 141 Consumer Credit Act 1974 applies (O 6 r 2(1)(e)). Section 141 gives exclusive jurisdiction to the county court to enforce a regulated agreement or a linked transaction. The definitions are complicated and are dealt with in a Practice Note set out in *The Supreme Court Practice* (1991) para 6/2/21. The county court's financial limit is currently £15,000.

5. Wrongful interference with goods

Order 15 r 10A(1) provides:

"Where the plaintiff in an action for wrongful interference with goods is one of two or more persons having or claiming any interest in the goods, then, unless he has the written authority of every other such person to sue on the latter's behalf, the writ or originating summons by which the action was begun shall be indorsed with a statement giving particulars of the plaintiff's title and identifying every other person who, to his knowledge, has or claims any interest in the goods."

6. Civil Jurisdiction and Judgments Act 1982

Order 6 r 1 (1)(b) provides:

"Where a claim made by the writ is one which the Court has power to hear and determine by virtue of the Civil Jurisdiction and Judgments Act 1982, the writ is indorsed before it is issued with a statement that the Court has power under that Act to hear and determine the claim, and that no proceedings involving the same cause of action are pending between the parties in Scotland, Northern Ireland or another Convention territory."

The indorsement is as follows:

This Court has power under and by virtue of the Civil Jurisdiction and Judgments Act 1982 to hear and determine the claim made in this writ and no proceedings involving the same cause of action are pending between the parties in Scotland, Northern Ireland or another Convention territory of any Contracting State as defined in section 1(3) of that Act.

7. Claims against the Crown

In the case of a Writ which begins civil proceedings against the Crown, the indorsement on the Writ must include a statement of the circumstances in which the Crown's liability is alleged to have arisen and as to the government department and officers of the Crown concerned (O 77 r 3(1)).

The effect of this rule is to require a slightly more detailed statement of the circumstances of the claim.

Example

The Plaintiff's claim is for damages for personal injuries suffered and loss and damage sustained when his right shoulder was injured on the 15th April 1990. The injury was caused by the negligence of the Defendant in requiring him to carry a Sharp Shooter automatic rifle which they knew or ought to have known was likely to cause the Plaintiff injury. At the time of the accident the Plaintiff was a guardsman stationed at Squaddy Barracks, London SW6. The Plaintiff's Solicitors have been in correspondence with the Ministry of Defence, Main Building, Whitehall, London SW1, and have received replies bearing the reference FRT/67589.

8. Personal injury actions

In relation to proceedings issued since 1 July 1991, the plaintiff in a personal injury case must indorse the Writ as follows:

This Writ includes a claim for personal injury but may be commenced in the High Court because the value of the action for the purposes of article 5 of the High Court and County Courts Jurisdiction Order 1991 exceeds £50,000.

9. Libel actions

By O 82 r 2, a Writ in a libel action must be indorsed with a statement giving sufficient particulars of the publications in respect of which the action is brought to enable them to be identified. The word "publications" means the documents containing the libel (eg newspapers, magazines, letters).

10. Mortgage actions

By O 88 r 3, the Writ or Originating Summons must be indorsed with or contain a statement showing:

    (a) where the mortgaged property is situated, and

    (b) if the plaintiff claims possession of the property and it is situated outside Greater London, whether the property consists of or includes a dwelling-house and, if so, whether the net annual value for rating of the property exceeds £1,000, and a certificate that the action is not one to which s 141 Consumer Credit Act 1974 applies.

In relation to domestic property (as defined by s 66 Local Government Finance Act 1988) the reference above to the net annual value for rating is to be construed as a reference to the value shown on the valuation list in force on 31 March 1990 or, if no such value was so shown, to its value by the year (ie the yearly market rental value).

11. Probate action

A Writ in a probate action must be indorsed with a statement of the nature of the interest of the plaintiff and of the defendant in the estate of the deceased to which the action relates (O 76 r 2(2)).

12. Indorsement as to capacity

Before a Writ is issued it must be indorsed:

(a) where the plaintiff sues in a representative capacity, with a statement of the capacity in which he sues;

(b) where the defendant is sued in a representative capacity, with a statement of the capacity in which he is sued (O 6 r 3).

Example

The Plaintiff's claim is on behalf of himself and all other members of the Clappleton Angling Club at 1234 Clappleton High Street, London SW15.

13. Indorsement as to place where cause of action arose

Where a Writ is to be issued out of a District Registry and any cause of action in respect of which relief is claimed by the Writ wholly or in part arose in a place in the district of that Registry, the Writ may be indorsed with a statement to that effect before it is issued (O 6 r 4).

Example

The cause of action in respect of which the Plaintiff claims relief in this action arose wholly or in part at Barchester, Yorkshire in the district of the District Registry named overleaf.

14. Indorsement as to solicitor and address

Order 6 r 5 provides:

"(1) Before a writ is issued, it must be indorsed –

(a) where the plaintiff sues by a solicitor, with the plaintiff's address and the solicitor's name or firm and a business address of his within the jurisdiction and also (if the solicitor is the agent of another) the name or firm and business address of his principal;

(b) where the plaintiff sues in person, with the address of his place of residence and, if his place of residence is not within the jurisdiction or if he has no place of residence, the address of a place within the jurisdiction at or to which documents for him may be delivered or sent."

Examples

This Writ was issued by Noggins & Co. of (address), Solicitors for the said Plaintiff whose address is (address).

This Writ was issued by Noggins & Co. of (address), Agent for Sendit & Co. of (address), Solicitors for the said Plaintiff whose address is (address).

Where the plaintiff sues in person:

This Writ was issued by the said Plaintiff who resides at (address).

If he has no place of residence within the jurisdiction:

This Writ was issued by the Plaintiff who resides at (address) and whose address for service is (address).

If counsel drafts the indorsement, his name should *not* appear on the Writ, since the indorsement is not a pleading.

15. Examples of claims

The following are examples of the brief form of claim which are indorsed on the Writ.

Damages for breach of contract

The Plaintiff's claim is for damages for breach of an oral contract made on or about the 14th day of September 1991 and interest pursuant to Section 35A of the Supreme Court Act 1981 at such rate and for such period as the Court thinks fit.

Damages for negligence

The Plaintiff's claim is for damages for personal injuries and loss and damage suffered as a result of the Defendant's negligence in driving a lorry in a road traffic accident on the 30th June 1991 at Richmond High Street, Surrey, and interest under Section 35A of the Supreme Court Act 1981 at such rate and for such period as the Court thinks fit.

Damages for nuisance

The Plaintiff's claim is for damages for nuisance caused by causing or permitting noise to disturb the enjoyment of the Plaintiff's premises at 134 Acacia Grove, Harpenden, Bedfordshire between the 2nd April 1990 and the 24th September 1991 and interest pursuant to Section 35A of the Supreme Court Act 1981 at such rate and for such period as the Court thinks fit.

Specific performance

The Plaintiff's claim is for specific performance of an agreement contained in a letter from the Plaintiff to the Defendant dated the 21st August 1991 and a copy of that letter signed by the Defendant on the 23rd August 1991 under which the Defendant agreed to restore the Plaintiff's Bentley motor car in consideration of the Plaintiff giving to the Defendant a Triumph motor car.

Injunction

The Plaintiff's claim is for an injunction to restrain the Defendant whether by himself, his servants or agents or otherwise howsoever, from trespassing on the Plaintiff's land at 134 Acacia Grove, Harpenden, Bedfordshire.

Declaration

The Plaintiff's claim is for a declaration that the Defendant is not entitled to forfeit a lease of the Plaintiff's premises at 134 Acacia Grove, Harpenden, Bedfordshire, dated the 4th November 1982.

Return of goods

The Plaintiff's claim is for the delivery up of a Renault 19 motor car registration no. F123DAP or its value and damages for wrongful interference thereof by its detention. The value of the motor car is £8,500.

Where more than one form of relief is sought, they should be divided into separately numbered paragraphs. For example:

The Plaintiff's claim is for:

1.   An injunction to restrain the Defendant whether by himself, his servants or agents or otherwise howsoever, from trespassing on the Plaintiff's land at 134 Acacia Grove, Harpenden, Bedfordshire.

2.   An order that the Defendant do forthwith remove so much of the wooden fencing as was erected on the Plaintiff's land.

3.   Damages for trespass.

4.   Interest pursuant to Section 35A of the Supreme Court Act 1981 at such rate and for such period as the Court thinks fit.

Chapter 5

Statement of Claim

The Statement of Claim is the first pleading to be served, and it is particularly important that it is well drafted, since it determines the form of subsequent pleadings. In the case of a simple debt claim, it might be only a few lines long. In a complex case, it could run to many pages.

1. Causes of action

Before starting to draft the Statement of Claim, it is necessary to identify the cause(s) of action which will form the basis of the claim. A "cause of action" consists of the facts which it is necessary for the plaintiff to prove to obtain the relief he seeks.

Examples

(a) A claim for damages for negligence (such as in a road traffic accident)

The plaintiff must prove (i) that the defendant owed him a duty of care, (ii) that the defendant breached the duty and (iii) that the plaintiff suffered damage as a result.

In order to prove (i), the Statement of Claim will have to set out the facts giving rise to a duty of care. In the case of a road accident, the facts that both plaintiff and defendant were road users will be sufficient.

To prove (ii), the Statement of Claim will have to make specific allegations of negligence against the defendant, eg that he was driving too fast, that he ignored a traffic sign, that he was not keeping a proper look-out for other road users.

To prove (iii), the Statement of Claim will have to allege that (in our example) as a result of the defendant's negligence, a collision occurred causing the plaintiff to be injured (setting out his injuries) and detailing any losses suffered.

(b) A claim for damages for breach of contract

The plaintiff must prove (i) that a binding contract was entered into, (ii) that the defendant was in breach of contract, and (iii) that the plaintiff suffered damage as a result.

To prove (i), the Statement of Claim will have to set out the relevant terms of and parties to the contract, how and when it was made, and the consideration.

To prove (ii), the Statement of Claim will have to give details of the breach(es) by the defendant.

To prove (iii), the Statement of Claim will have to set out details of the loss and damage suffered by the plaintiff.

(c) A claim for possession of land let on a tenancy

The plaintiff must prove (i) that he has title to the land and is entitled to possession, (ii) the terms of any agreement under which the defendant occupied the land, (iii) the termination of that agreement leading to the continued occupation of the land as being unlawful, and (iv) that there exist grounds for possession under any statute giving the defendant security.

If a Statement of Claim omits one or more facts necessary to establish a cause of action, it is liable to be struck out under O 18 r 19 as disclosing no reasonable cause of action.

If a Statement of Claim is not indorsed on the Writ, but is served separately, it must not contain any allegation or claim in respect of a cause of action unless that cause of action is mentioned in the Writ or arises from facts which are the same as, or include or form part of, facts giving rise to a cause of action so mentioned (O 18 r 15(2)). Subject to that, however, a plaintiff may in his Statement of Claim alter, modify or extend any claim made by him in the indorsement of the Writ without amending the indorsement.

The plaintiff may, of course, seek to amend the Writ to add or substitute a new cause of action, but if he does not do so, he cannot change the cause of action by the way the Statement of Claim is pleaded.

The plaintiff is not limited to pleading one cause of action in his Statement of Claim. Order 15 r 1 provides that he may in one action claim relief against the same defendant in respect of more than one cause of action:

> "(a) if the plaintiff claims, and the defendant is alleged to be liable, in the same capacity in respect of all the causes of action; or
>
> (b) if the plaintiff claims or the defendant is alleged to be liable in the capacity of executor or administrator of an estate in respect of one or more of the causes of action and in his personal capacity but with reference to the same estate in respect of all the others, or
>
> (c) with the leave of the Court."

However, O 15 r 1 is subject to O 15 r 5(1) which provides:

> "If claims in respect of two or more causes of action are included by a plaintiff in the same action or by a defendant in a counterclaim, or if two or more plaintiffs or defendants are parties to the same action, and it appears to the Court that the joinder of causes of action or of parties, as the case may be, may embarrass or delay the trial or is otherwise inconvenient, the Court may order separate trials or make such other order as may be expedient."

It is therefore desirable for the plaintiff to consider, before starting an action involving more than one cause of action, whether there is sufficient connection between them to justify including them all in a single set of proceedings.

2. The form of the Statement of Claim

We will start by looking at the various rules in O 18 which apply specifically to the Statement of Claim. As we have seen when considering the formal parts of a pleading, the Statement of Claim is divided into three parts: the heading, the body and the prayer.

(a) The heading

The Statement of Claim must state the date on which the Writ in the action was issued (O 18 r 15(3)). For obvious reasons, this does not apply to a Statement of Claim indorsed on the

Writ. In all other cases, the date of issue of the Writ must be given, and is conventionally stated in brackets immediately above the names of the parties, as follows:

IN THE HIGH COURT OF JUSTICE   **1991 B No. 1245**

QUEEN'S BENCH DIVISION

(Writ issued the 1st December 1990)

BETWEEN:

The words **STATEMENT OF CLAIM** appear in the middle of the page immediately following the names of the parties.

(b) The body

(i) Introductory paragraph

It is usual to start a Statement of Claim of any length with an introductory paragraph (or two) to "set the scene". Typically, this will describe the status of any party which is relevant.

Examples

(a) The claim is for damages for breach of a contract for the sale of goods. The fact that the defendant is running a business selling the goods in question is relevant to establishing the implied terms.

IN THE HIGH COURT OF JUSTICE   **1991 S No. 4567**

QUEEN'S BENCH DIVISION

BETWEEN: JONATHAN SQUELCH   <u>Plaintiff</u>

and

SILVERTONGUE FURNISHINGS LIMITED <u>Defendant</u>

STATEMENT OF CLAIM

1.   The Defendant company is in business as a specialist supplier of antique and reproduction furniture, and trades, inter alia, from a showroom at 250 High Street, Barchester, Wiltshire.

(b) The claim is for damages for negligence arising out of a road traffic accident. The proposed defendant is the employer of the driver who drove negligently and the claim is brought on the basis of vicarious liability.

IN THE HIGH COURT OF JUSTICE 1991 S No. 4567

QUEEN'S BENCH DIVISION

BETWEEN: JONATHAN SQUELCH Plaintiff

and

SILVERTONGUE FURNISHINGS LIMITED Defendant

STATEMENT OF CLAIM

1. At all material times the Defendant employed one Peter Johnson as a van driver.

2. At about 4 p.m. on the 15th February 1991, the Plaintiff was crossing Oak Lane, Barchester, Wiltshire, opposite the Post Office, when a Ford Transit van, registration number P145 RTA, being driven by the said Johnson in the course of his said employment struck the Plaintiff.

3. The said accident was caused by the negligence of the said Johnson.

PARTICULARS

etc.

(c) The plaintiff wishes to claim possession of a shop let to the defendant, and pleads his title.

IN THE HIGH COURT OF JUSTICE 1991 H No. 9486

CHANCERY DIVISION

BETWEEN: HAPPY LETTING PLC Plaintiff

and

SILVERTONGUE FURNISHINGS LIMITED Defendant

STATEMENT OF CLAIM

1. The Plaintiff is the freehold owner and entitled to possession of the premises known as and situate at 250 High Street, Barchester, Wiltshire, hereinafter called "the premises".

As we have already seen, the parties should be referred to in the body of the pleading by their description, Plaintiff, First

Defendant, Second Defendant etc. In the case of a very long Statement of Claim with many parties, it may be clearer for the reader if a form of abbreviated names is used. The first paragraph will then be in the form of a table defining the names used. It is emphasised that this must only be done where it is really necessary.

Example

IN THE HIGH COURT OF JUSTICE   1991 S No. 7869

QUEEN'S BENCH DIVISION

BETWEEN:
　　　　　　　　　　(1) STRAPPERS BANK PLC
　　　　　　　　　　(2) FALLOUT LIMITED
　　　　　　　　　　(3) ZACHARIAH THOMPSON   <u>Plaintiffs</u>
　　　　　　　　　　　　　　and
　　　　　　　　　　(1) HANDOUT BANK PLC
　　　　　　　　　　(2) GUMBOOT TUNNEL SA
　　　　　　　　　(3) GLOOMY INTERIORS LIMITED
　　　　　　　　　　(4) VIOLET CARSTAIRS
　　　　　　　　　　(5) GEORGE NICHOLSON   <u>Defendants</u>

STATEMENT OF CLAIM

1.　In this Statement of Claim, the parties will be referred to as follows:–

The First Plaintiff as "Strappers"

The Second Plaintiff as "Fallout"

The Third Plaintiff as "Mr. Thompson"

The First Defendant as "Handout"

The Second Defendant as "Gumboot"

The Third Defendant as "Gloomy"

The Fourth Defendant as "Mrs. Carstairs"

The Fifth Defendant as "Mr. Nicholson".

It is obviously desirable that the subsequent pleadings use the same system, otherwise confusion reigns.

Sometimes it is not until pleadings are further advanced that the benefits of referring to the parties in this way becomes apparent, for example if one or more third parties are brought in, and they wish to bring in other parties and/or defendants wish to counterclaim against existing and other parties.

(ii) The story

The rest of the body of the Statement of Claim tells the story of the claim from the plaintiff's point of view.

There is one specific limitation on the cause of action which may be pleaded. The Statement of Claim must not contain any allegation or claim in respect of a cause of action unless that cause of action is mentioned in the Writ or arises from facts which are the same as, or include or form part of, facts giving rise to a cause of action so mentioned (O 18 r 15(2)). Subject to that, a plaintiff may in his Statement of Claim alter, modify or extend any claim made by him in the indorsement of the Writ without amending the indorsement.

One of the effects of this rule, which applies when the Statement of Claim is served after the Writ is issued (ie, not indorsed on it), is to prevent the plaintiff relying on a cause of action which accrued after the Writ was issued. For example, where a claim depends on the expiry of a notice (eg, a notice to terminate a contract, or a notice to quit land) and the expiry occurs after the Writ was issued, it is too late to rely on the notice in the Statement of Claim, and fresh proceedings will have to be issued.

The pleading is set out chronologically, and each allegation must, if possible, be contained in a separate paragraph. It is easiest to see how this should be done by looking at an example. Example (b) above can be continued thus:

IN THE HIGH COURT OF JUSTICE　　　　　　　**1991 S No. 4567**
QUEEN'S BENCH DIVISION
BETWEEN:　　　　　　　JONATHAN SQUELCH　　　　<u>Plaintiff</u>
　　　　　　　　　　　　　　　and
　　　　　　　SILVERTONGUE FURNISHINGS LIMITED　　<u>Defendant</u>

STATEMENT OF CLAIM

1.　At all material times the Defendant employed one Peter Johnson as a van driver.

2.　At about 4 p.m. on the 15th February 1991, the Plaintiff was crossing Oak Lane, Barchester, Wiltshire opposite the Post Office, when a Ford Transit van, registration number P145 RTA, being driven by the said Johnson in the course of his said employment struck the Plaintiff.

45

3. The said accident was caused by the negligence of the said Johnson.

PARTICULARS OF NEGLIGENCE

(a) Driving too fast in all the circumstances;

(b) Failing to keep any, or any proper lookout;

(c) Failing to brake, steer or otherwise control the said van so as to avoid colliding with the Plaintiff.

(d) On the 28th April 1991, at Barchester Magistrates' Court, the said Johnson was convicted of driving without due care and attention as a result of the incident pleaded in Paragraph 2 hereof. He was fined £100 and his licence was indorsed with 4 penalty points. The conviction is relevant to the issue of his negligence, and the Plaintiff intends to rely upon it.

4. By reason of the said accident, the Plaintiff suffered pain and injury, loss and damage

PARTICULARS OF INJURY

(i) Compound fracture of the right tibia;

(ii) Bruising to the face;

(iii) Shock.

The Plaintiff was born on the 4th May 1954.

PARTICULARS OF SPECIAL DAMAGE

(i)	Cost of trousers damaged beyond repair	£45
(ii)	Taxi fares to hospital 3 @ £10	30
(iii)	4 weeks net loss of pay @ £200/wk	800
	Total	£875

5. Further, the Plaintiff is entitled to and claims interest on such damages as he is awarded pursuant to Section 35A of the Supreme Court Act 1981 at such rate and for such period as this Honourable Court shall think fit.

AND the Plaintiff claims damages and the said interest to be assessed.

Served . . .

The following points should be noted:

- Paragraph 2 sets out the facts of the accident in almost completely neutral terms. The defendant could admit this paragraph in its Defence without admitting liability. It is a good idea to set out what are expected to be the non-contentious parts of the case in paragraphs that can be admitted by the other side. This assists in identifying what is really in dispute.

- Paragraph 3 deals with the nitty gritty, the allegations of negligence. The allegations are made against the driver, not the defendant; we have already fixed the defendant with liability by pleading the facts giving rise to vicarious liability.

- Each allegation of negligence is separate and precise. "Failing to keep any or any proper lookout" might be thought to be a little long-winded, but strictly speaking an allegation of failing to keep *any* lookout could be defeated by evidence that the driver kept *some* lookout. Make sure that all the allegations are justified, and are not just put in as fillers.

- The particulars of injury and special damage are brief and to the point. These matters will be amplified in the medical reports and schedule served with the Statement of Claim; however, it is still necessary to plead them, and it is not sufficient to say simply "Refer to the report served with the Statement of Claim".

(c) The prayer

At the end of the Statement of Claim comes the prayer, which must set out specifically the relief or remedy which the plaintiff claims (O 18 r 15(1)). Costs need not be specifically claimed, and it is generally thought to be good practice to omit costs from the prayer in the Queen's Bench Division and the county court. In the Chancery Division costs are claimed in the prayer as well as "Further or other relief".

The prayer starts:

AND the Plaintiff claims:

and continues with the different remedies sought. Where more than one form of relief is sought, they should be divided into separate numbered paragraphs.

Common remedies are:

- (i) A specified sum of money, eg a claim on a loan, the price of goods sold and delivered.
- (ii) Damages for, eg negligence, nuisance, breach of contract. Although special damages are set out in the

body of the pleading, the prayer will simply seek "Damages" as an unquantified figure.

(iii) An injunction, either negative (restraining the defendant from doing a specified act) or mandatory (requiring the defendant to do something). The prayer should set out precisely the terms of the injunction that is sought.

(iv) A declaration. Again, the prayer should set out precisely the terms sought.

(v) Specific performance of a contract.

(vi) An account, eg of profits made by the defendant, and an order that the defendant pay to the plaintiff any sums found to be due.

(vii) Possession of land, eg by a landlord against a former tenant. The land should be clearly identified in the prayer. Claims for possession usually also involve claims for rent arrears, mesne profits etc.

(viii) The appointment of a receiver.

(ix) Interest (see Chapter 2).

Just as a plaintiff may plead alternative inconsistent allegations in the body of his Statement of Claim, he may also claim alternative inconsistent forms of relief in the prayer, provided it is made clear how the case is put.

If there is more than one defendant, different forms of relief can be claimed against each. For example:

AND the Plaintiff claims against the First Defendant:

1. Possession of 145 High Street, Brokerville, Surrey;

Against the Second Defendant:

2. Damages for breach of covenant;

3. Interest thereon under paragraph 12 hereof to be assessed.

If the same relief is claimed against both of two defendants, who are alleged to be jointly and severally liable, the prayer will say, for example:

AND the Plaintiff claims against the Defendants and each of them:

1. An injunction restraining them by themselves, their servants or agents or otherwise howsoever, from soliciting or attempting to solicit custom from any of the Plaintiff's existing clients for a period of 12 months from the 1st June 1991;

2. The said sum of £15,600;

3. Interest thereon under paragraph 13 hereof, amounting to £2114.89 to the date hereof and continuing at the daily rate of £ . . . until judgment or sooner payment.

Similarly, if two plaintiffs claim the same relief, the prayer will start:

AND the Plaintiffs and each of them claim: . . .

Chapter 6

Particulars of pleading

Order 18 contains a number of rules setting out which allegations must be particularised in pleadings. The rules which apply to all pleadings are considered in this chapter, and are also referred to, as necessary, in the chapters dealing with Statements of Claim, Defences etc. The rules dealing with the required contents of specific pleadings are considered in the relevant chapter.

Order 18 r 12 is the most important rule; it sets out which matters must be particularised. It is dealt with in this book as amended with effect from 4 June 1990. In relation to a pleading served before that date, the previous r 12(1) applies — for the text of the old rule, see *The Supreme Court Practice 1988*.

By O 18 r 12(1), subject to r 12(2), every pleading must contain the necessary particulars of any claim, defence or other matter pleaded, including, without prejudice to the generality of the foregoing:

(a) particulars of any misrepresentation, fraud, breach of trust, wilful default, or undue influence on which the party pleading relies;

(b) where a party pleading alleges any condition of the mind of any person, whether any disorder or disability of mind or any malice, fraud, fraudulent intention or other condition of mind except knowledge, particulars of the facts on which the party relies; and

(c) where a claim for damages is made against a party pleading, particulars of any facts on which the party relies in mitigation of, or otherwise in relation to, the amount of damages.

Rule 12(2) provides that where it is necessary to give particulars of debt, expenses or damages and those particulars exceed three folios, they must be set out in a separate document referred to in the pleading, and the pleading must state whether the document has already been served and, if so, when, or is to be served with the pleading.

Order 1 r 4(1) defines "folio" as meaning 72 words, each figure being counted as one word. Consequently, by use of this quaint formula, a separate schedule of debt, expenses or damages must be used if particulars would exceed 216 words or figures.

Example

> The Defendant owes the Plaintiff the total sum of £100,000. Particulars of how the said sum is made up are contained in a Statement of Account dated the 1st November 1990, which exceeds three folios, [and which was sent to the Defendant on the 15th November 1990 *or*, a copy of which is served herewith].

The remainder of O 18 r 12 deals with documents which must be served with a Statement of Claim in a personal injury action (see below) and further and better particulars (see page 56 *et seq*).

Order 18 r 8(3) requires a claim for exemplary or provisional damages to be specifically pleaded, together with the facts on which the party pleading relies.

Any claim for interest must be specifically pleaded, whether under s 35A Supreme Court Act 1981, or otherwise. For the pleading of interest, see Chapter 4.

The following is a list of some of the matters which must be particularised, by virtue of express rules or decided cases:

Adultery	Disorder or disability of the mind
Aggravated damages	Exemplary damages
Agreement	Fair comment
Breach of duty	Fraud
Breach of trust	Fraudulent intention
Consideration	Illegality
Conspiracy	Intention
Contributory negligence	Interest
Damages	Knowledge
Dishonesty	Limitation

Malice	Provisional damages
Misrepresentation	Release
Mitigation of damage	Special damage
Negligence	Undue influence
Performance	Wilful default

It is O 18 r 12(1) which gives teeth to the system of pleadings described in Chapter 1, and ensures that the other side knows what case they have to meet. It is desirable that, at least in the matters set out in r 12(1)(a) to (c), the pleading should specify particulars of the allegation under a special heading. The heading will be in the middle of the page and will say **PARTICULARS OF**...

Example

The allegation is that the plaintiff was induced to buy from the defendant a house suffering from damp, in reliance upon the defendant's representation that it was free of damp.

. . .

3.   By letter dated the 1st February 1990, the Defendant, in order to induce the Plaintiff to purchase the said premises, represented that the said premises were free from damp.

4.   In reliance upon the said representation, the Plaintiff purchased the said premises on the 1st March 1990 for £100,000.

5.   The Defendant's said representation was false and was made fraudulently, in that the Defendant knew that it was false, or made it recklessly, not caring whether it was true or false.

PARTICULARS OF FALSITY

The said premises were not free from damp, but suffer from extensive rising damp in all external walls.

PARTICULARS OF FRAUD

On the 15th January 1990 the Defendant received a report from Chekitover Limited, commissioned by him, and specifying in detail the said rising damp affecting the said premises.

The desirability of setting out particulars under a separate heading is not confined to the matters listed in r 12(1).

1. Rules for specific causes of action

(a) Personal injury actions

The general rule, which applies to cases where the Writ was

issued after 4 June 1990, is that the plaintiff must serve with his Statement of Claim:

- a medical report; and
- a statement of the special damages claimed.

"Medical report" is defined as a report substantiating all the personal injuries alleged in the Statement of Claim which the plaintiff proposes to adduce in evidence as part of his case at the trial.

"A statement of the special damages claimed" is defined as a statement giving full particulars of the special damages claimed for expenses and losses already incurred and an estimate of any future expenses and losses (including loss of earnings and of pension rights).

The following two points should be noted:

- Injuries and special damages must still be pleaded, as before, in the Statement of Claim. It is the author's view that this rule does not allow a plaintiff simply to refer to the medical report as his Particulars of Injury.
- If the injuries or special damages change between the time of service of the Statement of Claim and the trial, care must be taken to ensure that the Statement of Claim, the medical report and the statement of damages are amended to reflect the current position.

If the documents are not served with the Statement of Claim, the court may either specify a time within which they must be provided, or make such other order as it thinks fit (including dispensing with the requirement, or staying the proceedings).

(b) Provisional damages

Both the Particulars of Injury and the prayer must make the claim for provisional damages clear, and set out all the relevant facts which need to be proved under s 32A Supreme Court Act 1981.

Example

After the Particulars of Injury:

The injuries set out, and the claim for special damages and future loss do not take into account the chance that at some definite or indefinite time in the future the Plaintiff will, as a result of the Defendant's said negligence, develop some serious disease, namely grand mal epilepsy.

In the event of an award of provisional damages being refused, the Plaintiff contends that such chance of further serious disease includes a risk of approximatley 5% of it occurring. If so he would require exploratory surgery, and be permanently on drugs to control it. He would be unable to enjoy his hobby of motor racing.

The prayer:

AND the Plaintiff claims:

1. Damages on the assumption that the Plaintiff will not at a future date as a result of the Defendant's said negligence, develop the following serious disease, namely grand mal epilepsy;

2. An order that if at a future date the Plaintiff develops such a condition he shall be entitled to apply for further damages;

3. Interest thereon pursuant to Section 35A of the Supreme Court Act 1981 to be assessed.

(c) Defamation actions

Three matters are dealt with in O 82 r 3. They apply equally where there is a counterclaim, with the necessary changes to the parties:

(i) Innuendo

Where the plaintiff alleges that the words or matters complained of were used in a defamatory sense other than their ordinary meaning, he must give particulars of the facts and matters on which he relies in support of such sense.

(ii) "Rolled-up" plea

Where the defendant alleges that, in so far as words complained of consist of statements of fact, they are true in substance and in fact, and in so far as they consist of expressions of opinion, they are fair comment on a matter of public interest, or pleads to the like effect, he must give particulars stating which of the words complained of he alleges are statements of fact and of the facts and matters he relies on in support of the allegation that the words are true.

(iii) Malice

Where the plaintiff alleges that the defendant maliciously

published the words or matters complained of, he need not in his Statement of Claim give particulars of the facts on which he relies in support of the allegation of malice, but if the defendant pleads that any of those words or matters are fair comment on the matter of public interest or were published upon a privileged occasion and the plaintiff intends to allege that the defendant was actuated by express malice, he must serve a Reply giving particulars of the fact and matters from which the malice is to be inferred.

(d) Contentious probate proceedings

In relation to the contents of the pleadings, O 76 r 9 provides that:

  (i) Where the plaintiff disputes the interest of a defendant, he must allege in the Statement of Claim that he denies the interest of that defendant.

  (ii) In a probate action in which the interest by virtue of which a party claims to be entitled to a grant of letters of administration is disputed, the party disputing that interest must show in his pleading that, if the allegations made therein are proved, he would be entitled to an interest in the estate.

  (iii) Without prejudice to O 18 r 7, any party who pleads that at the time when a will, the subject of the action, was alleged to have been executed the testator did not know and approve of its contents, must specify the nature of the case on which he intends to rely, and no allegation in support of that plea which would be relevant in support of any of the following other pleas, that is to say:

    (a) that the will was not duly executed,

    (b) that at the time of the execution of the will the testator was not of sound mind, memory and understanding, and

    (c) that the execution of the will was obtained by undue influence or fraud,

shall be made by that party unless that other plea is also pleaded.

(e) Fatal accident claims

By s 2(4) Fatal Accidents Act 1976 (as substituted by the Administration of Justice Act 1982), the plaintiff is required to deliver to the defendant or his solicitor full particulars (i) of the persons for whom and on whose behalf the action is brought, and (ii) of the nature of the claim in respect of which damages are sought to be recovered.

An example is given in Appendix B at page 163.

2. Further and Better Particulars

If a party is faced with a pleading which is not sufficiently particularised, he may make a request for particulars. Before making a request, consideration should be given to the question whether the provision of particulars will really help the case of the person seeking them. Sometimes, it is tactically preferable to leave the other side's pleadings in an inadequate state; they may have overlooked something important, and a request for particulars might alert them to it − or, at trial, they may be forced to amend and to give particulars necessitating an adjournment at their expense.

The rules encourage the party seeking particulars to make an application by letter first. If this is not done, the court may refuse to make an order that particulars be given (O 18 r 12(6)).

If a letter does not have the required effect, a formal pleaded request is made. The Request for Further and Better Particulars must identify the paragraph and words in the pleading of which particulars are sought, and be drafted clearly, so that a precise answer can be given. Frequently, a number of questions in sequence are asked.

Example

The claim is for damages for breach of a contract for the sale of a car. Paragraph 3 of the Statement of Claim has alleged "It was a term of the contract that the car had travelled no more than 10,000 miles". This is obviously inadequate, since the pleading does not say whether the term was express or implied or how it came to be incorporated into the contract.

The form is as follows:

IN THE HIGH COURT OF JUSTICE   1991 J No. 7863

QUEEN'S BENCH DIVISION

BETWEEN: DEAN JAMES   <u>Plaintiff</u>
                                and
                    BENT AUTOS LIMITED   <u>Defendant</u>

REQUEST FOR FURTHER AND BETTER PARTICULARS OF THE STATEMENT OF CLAIM

<u>Under Paragraph 3</u>

Of "It was a term of the contract . . ."

State

1.   Whether the term was express or implied;
2.   If express,
     (i)   whether it was written or oral;
     (ii)   If written, identify every document relied upon and the words used therein;
     (iii) If oral, state who agreed the term on behalf of each party, the words used, and the time and place of any conversation;
3.   If implied, state all facts and matters relied upon in support of the contention that such a term should be implied into the contract.

Served the 15th day of April 1991.

In answering the Request, the form of Further and Better Particulars must include the requests themselves, with each reply following immediately after the corresponding request (O 18 r 12(7)). In our example, there is only one request, and the form of reply is as follows:

IN THE HIGH COURT OF JUSTICE   1991 J No. 7863

QUEEN'S BENCH DIVISION

BETWEEN: DEAN JAMES   <u>Plaintiff</u>
                                and
                    BENT AUTOS LIMITED   <u>Defendant</u>

FURTHER AND BETTER PARTICULARS OF THE STATEMENT OF CLAIM PURSUANT TO REQUEST SERVED THE 15TH APRIL 1991

<u>Request</u>

<u>Under Paragraph 3</u>

Of "It was a term of the contract . . ."

State

1. Whether the term was express or implied;

2. If express,
   (i) whether it was written or oral;
   (ii) If written, identify every document relied upon and the words used therein;
   (iii) If oral, state who agreed the term on behalf of each party, the words used, and the time and place of any conversation;

3. If implied, state all facts and matters relied upon in support of the contention that such a term should be implied into the contract.

<u>Reply</u>

1. Express;

2. (i) Oral;
   (ii) Not applicable;
   (iii) The Plaintiff and Joseph Twister, the manager of the Defendant's showroom. The Plaintiff said to the said Twister words to the effect "Is the clock accurate, it only shows 10,000 miles?" and the said Twister said "It sure is, I'd stake my life on it." The conversation took place at the Defendant's showroom at 56 Monoxide Lane, Manchester, on the 3rd January 1991 at about 11 a.m. shortly before the Plaintiff signed the sale documents.

3. Not applicable.

Served the 24th day of May 1991.

If particulars are not given voluntarily, "the Court may order a party to serve on any other party particulars of any claim, defence or other matter stated in his pleading, or in any affidavit of his ordered to stand as a pleading, or a statement of the nature of the case on which he relies, and the order may be made on such terms as the Court thinks just" (O 18 r 12(3)).

Note that the rule provides for a party to be ordered to state the nature of his case if this is not clear.

Without prejudice to the generality of r 12(3), O 18 r 12(4) provides that where a party alleges as a fact that a person had knowledge or notice of some fact, matter or thing, the court may order that party to serve on any other party:

(a) where he alleges knowledge, particulars of the facts on which he relies, and

(b) where he alleges notice, particulars of the notice.

It is not sufficient to allege that the other party must know the facts better than his opponent. Each party is entitled to know the case to be made against him.

Particulars before Defence

As a delaying tactic, a defendant may seek an order for further and better particulars of the Statement of Claim so as to put off having to serve his Defence. An order for particulars cannot be made before service of the Defence "unless, in the opinion of the Court, the order is necessary or desirable to enable the defendant to plead or for some other special reason" (O 18 r 12(5)).

Chapter 7

The Defence

Once a Statement of Claim is served on a defendant, he must reply by serving a Defence. Failure to do so will result in a judgment being entered in default. Usually, the Defence is the only pleading served by a defendant, and it is particularly important that it is drafted with care.

1. Principles

The following principles should be borne in mind:

(a) It is necessary to deal with each allegation pleaded in the Statement of Claim. This is because (subject to an exception, for which, see below) any allegation of fact contained in a Statement of Claim is deemed to be admitted unless it is traversed in the Defence (O 18 r 13(1)).

(b) There are three basic ways of dealing with an allegation in the Statement of Claim: it may be admitted, denied or not admitted. A denial or non-admission is called a "traverse" (O 18 r 13(2)).

(c) If an allegation of fact is admitted in the Defence, it is deemed to be proved at trial, and no evidence need be called to establish it. So far as the plaintiff is concerned, there is no effective difference between a denial and a non-admission; in both cases, he will need to prove his allegation by calling evidence. The distinction from the defendant's point of view is really one of emphasis: he will deny an allegation which is genuinely in dispute, and not admit one which he

60

requires the plaintiff to prove formally, usually because it is outside the defendant's knowledge.

(d) All defences relied upon must be pleaded. This is merely an example of the rule that a party's case at trial is limited by its pleadings.

(e) There is no objection (indeed it is commonplace) to pleading alternative, inconsistent defences. Thus, for example, in a Defence to a claim for damages for breach of contract, a defendant can plead (i) there was no contract, (ii) if there was, there was no breach, (iii) if there was a breach, no damage was suffered.

(f) A general denial does not operate as a sufficient traverse (O 18 r 13(3)). Some people seem to believe that an effective delaying tactic is to serve a Defence saying simply "The Statement of Claim is denied in its entirety" or "Each and every allegation in the Statement of Claim is denied". This is sometimes referred to as a "holding defence". However, it should never be used, since it is liable to be struck out as not disclosing a defence. The correct course of action if more time is needed (for instance, to obtain instructions) is to request an extension of time from the other side, or if that is refused, to issue a "time summons", seeking more time from the court.

Person under disability: The exception to principle (a) above concerns a person under disability, ie a minor or mental patient. Such a person is not to be taken to admit the truth of any allegation of fact made in the pleading of the opposite party by reason only that he has not traversed it in his pleadings (O 80 r 8). This does not, however, prevent a person under disability from making a valid express admission.

2. Form of Defence

A Defence must, of course, comply with the formal requirements applicable to all pleadings, as set out in Chapter 1. After the heading, the word DEFENCE appears in the middle of the page. If there is more than one defendant, the description of the pleading should make it clear whose Defence it is, thus:

With one defendant:

61

IN THE HIGH COURT OF JUSTICE   1991 A No. 123

QUEEN'S BENCH DIVISION

BETWEEN: JOHN ANDREWS   <u>Plaintiff</u>

                                            and

                                  PETER SMITH   <u>Defendant</u>

DEFENCE

With more than one defendant:

IN THE HIGH COURT OF JUSTICE   1991 A No. 123

QUEEN'S BENCH DIVISION

BETWEEN: JOHN ANDREWS   <u>Plaintiff</u>

                                            and

                                  (1) PETER SMITH

                                  (2) ALAN JOHNSON

                                  (3) SAVE-US LIMITED   <u>Defendants</u>

DEFENCE OF SECOND AND THIRD DEFENDANTS

3. Contents of Defence

Chapter 6 sets out certain matters which must be pleaded in detail. As with the Statement of Claim, the rules set out a number of requirements specifically for Defences.

By O 18 r 8(1), a party must in any pleading subsequent to a Statement of Claim plead specifically any matter, for example performance, release, the expiry of the relevant period of limitation, fraud, or any fact showing illegality:

(a) which he alleges makes any claim or defence of the opposite party not maintainable; or

(b) which, if not specifically pleaded, might take the opposite party by surprise; or

(c) which raises issues of fact not arising out of the preceding pleading.

This spells out the obligation on a defendant to make the nature of his Defence clear to the plaintiff in advance of the trial. Take, as an example, a Statement of Claim which alleges that the plaintiff was injured in a road accident caused by the negligent driving of the defendant. The defendant knows that he was responsible for the accident and the plaintiff's injuries, but wishes to rely upon the Limitation Act 1980, since the accident took place 3½ years before the Writ was issued. It is not sufficient for him simply to deny liability. He must admit the accident, and plead reliance on the relevant provisions of the Limitation Act. This is an example of what is called "confession and avoidance". The defendant admits the facts pleaded, but puts forward further matters as his defence.

Order 18 r 8(2) states that without prejudice to r 8(1), a defendant to an action for the recovery of land must plead specifically every ground of defence on which he relies, and a plea that he is in possession of the land by himself or his tenant is not sufficient (thus reversing an old rule).

Order 18 r 12(1)(c) provides that where a claim for damages is made against a party pleading, particulars of any facts on which the party relies in mitigation of, or otherwise in relation to, the amount of damages must be pleaded. This rule has applied to any pleading served since 4 June 1990, and reverses the preceding practice whereby the amount of damages was automatically deemed to be traversed.

(a) Tender

Order 18 r 16 provides that where a defence of tender before action is pleaded, the defendant must pay into court in accordance with O 22 the amount alleged to have been tendered, and the tender is not available as a defence unless and until payment into court has been made.

(b) Set-off

Where a claim by a defendant to a sum of money (whether of an ascertained amount or not) is relied on as a defence to the whole or part of a claim made by the plaintiff, it may be included in the Defence and set-off against the plaintiff's claim, whether or not it is also added as a Counterclaim (O 18 r 17).

In practice, in most cases where set-off is pleaded, the defendant seeks to set-off against the plaintiff's claim that which he recovers under a Counterclaim, in extinction or diminution of the plaintiff's claim. A form of words such as the following sentence is pleaded at the end of the Defence:

> Further or alternatively, the Defendant claims to set-off against the Plaintiff's claim such sums as he is awarded upon his counterclaim herein in extinction or diminution thereof.

4. Style of Defence

The recommended way in which to plead a Defence is to deal with the Statement of Claim paragraph by paragraph, answering each allegation of fact separately. There are two overwhelming advantages to this practice over any other:

(a) The parties and the court can see clearly which facts are in dispute, and which are admitted. The issues for trial are thus plainly defined.

(b) It minimises the danger of a defendant inadvertently omitting to reply to an allegation in the Statement of Claim, thus resulting in it being deemed admitted (by virtue of O 18 r 13(1)).

In order to avoid the danger referred to in (b), it is common practice to insert at the end of the Defence a general traverse in the following or similar form:

> Save as is hereinbefore expressly admitted, each and every allegation contained in the Statement of Claim is denied as if the same had been set out herein and specifically traversed seriatim.

The word "seriatim" means "separately and in order". However, it is not good style to use the general traverse when the Statement of Claim is short and all the allegations have clearly been dealt with in the Defence. Furthermore, the general traverse does not allow a defendant to avoid the rules requiring specific matters of defence to be properly pleaded.

The recommended method of pleading a Defence cannot be adopted in two cases:

(a) Where the Statement of Claim is poorly drafted, so that the "story" is not told chronologically or clearly enough to be answered step by step. In that case it may be necessary to plead the Defence by setting out the defendant's account of what happened, and then stating why the plaintiff's claim is denied.

(b) Where the Statement of Claim is merely a one paragraph claim, for example for money due under an invoice in respect of goods sold and delivered. In those circumstances, the Defence must set out a chronological set of events.

Example

The Statement of Claim is indorsed on the Writ. It says:

The Plaintiff's claim is for the price of goods sold and delivered by the Plaintiff to the Defendant at the Defendant's request, as per the Plaintiff's invoice, totalling £4,000, which have been supplied to the Defendant.

PARTICULARS

Invoice no. 1234 dated 1st December 1990	£1,000
Invoice no. 2345 dated 15th December 1990	£1,000
Invoice no. 3456 dated 21st January 1991	£1,000
Invoice no. 4567 dated 23rd February 1991	£1,000
	£4,000

The Plaintiff further claims interest on the said sum pursuant to Section 35A of the Supreme Court Act 1981 at 15% per annum from the 23rd February 1991 to the date hereof, amounting to £98.63 and continuing at the daily rate of £1.64.

AND the Plaintiff claims:

1. £4,000

2. Interest amounting to £98.63 to date and continuing at the rate of £1.64 per day until judgment or sooner payment.

After the heading, the Defence should read as follows:

DEFENCE

1. The Plaintiff manufactures and supplies lawnmowers. The Defendant owns a garden centre.

2. On various dates between 1st October and the 25th December 1990, the Defendant ordered by telephone a number of lawnmowers from the Plaintiff at a cost of £100 each.

3. It was an implied condition of the said agreement that the lawnmowers would be of merchantable quality and reasonably fit for their purpose, namely for cutting grass.

4. The Plaintiff's claim relates to invoices sent to the Defendant in respect of lawnmowers allegedly supplied to them. In respect of each invoice pleaded, the Defendant's case is as follows:

   (i) Invoice nos. 1234 and 4567 — none of the 20 lawnmowers the subject of these 2 invoices was delivered to the Defendant.

   (ii) Invoice nos. 2345 and 3456 — these related to 2 orders for a total of 20 lawnmowers delivered to the Defendant on the 12th December 1990. Upon inspection, it was discovered that none of them had any blades fitted. The Defendant telephoned the Plaintiff on the 13th December 1990 to inform him of this fact and to reject the lawnmowers. The Plaintiff agreed to send a lorry to collect them within a week. The Plaintiff has failed to collect the lawnmowers, which remain at the Defendant's premises.

5. In the premises, it is denied that the Plaintiff is entitled to the relief claimed or any relief.

Served the 15th day of July 1991.

Note how the plaintiff's claim is first mentioned in paragraph 4 of the Defence, and fits into the narrative in a logical place.

As has been mentioned, the conventional way of pleading a Defence when faced with a lengthier Statement of Claim is to deal with the allegations paragraph by paragraph. The following are two examples of a defence to a claim for possession of rented property on the ground of non-payment of rent:

IN THE HIGH COURT OF JUSTICE   **1991 E No. 6857**

QUEEN'S BENCH DIVISION

BETWEEN: EYESORE PROPERTY LIMITED   <u>Plaintiff</u>
                           and
                    JOHN LITTLE   <u>Defendant</u>

STATEMENT OF CLAIM

1. The Plaintiff is the owner and entitled to possession of the premises known as 35 The Grove, Brokerville, in the County of Surrey, hereinafter called "the premises".

2. By a lease dated the 15th October 1987 Johnson Lettings Limited let the premises to the Defendant for the term of 20 years from the 29th September 1987 at a rent of £10,000 per annum for the first 10 years of the term (and thereafter subject

to review) payable quarterly in advance on the usual quarter days.

3. By Clause 2 of the said lease, the Defendant covenanted:
   (i) to pay the rent on the days and in the manner specified;
   (ii) if the said rent should be in arrears for 14 days after falling due, to pay interest on the said rent at 15% per annum from the day the same fell due until actual payment.

4. Clause 4 of the said lease contained a proviso for re-entry in the event, inter alia, that the said rent should be in arrears and unpaid for 21 days after falling due.

5. In March 1988 the reversion immediately expectant upon the determination of the said term became vested in the Plaintiff.

6. The Defendant is in arrears of rent in the sum of £7,500, being the quarters falling due on the 25th December 1990, the 25th March 1991 and the 24th June 1991.

7. By reason of the said arrears, the said lease has become and is hereby forfeited to the Plaintiff.

8. No part of the premises comprises a dwelling-house.

9. The Plaintiff claims interest on the said arrears under the said lease at 15% per annum as follows:

   On £2,500 from 25th December 1990 to 24th March 1991 –
   £93.49
   On £5,000 from 25th March 1991 to 24th June 1991 –
   £186.99
   On £7,500 from 25th June 1991 to date hereof –   £77.05
   Total   £357.53

And continuing at the daily rate of £3.08 until judgment or sooner payment.

AND the Plaintiff claims:

1. Possession of the premises;

2. Arrears of rent of £7,500;

3. Interest thereon under Paragraph 9 hereof amounting to £357.53 to the date hereof and continuing at the daily rate of £3.08 until judgment or sooner payment.

In the following example, the defendant puts forward two defences. As to the first quarter's rent claimed, he says he paid it to the Plaintiff's agent. As to the remaining two, he claims to have tendered the rent, which was refused. As we have seen, this defence requires the defendant to pay the tendered amount into court under O 18 r 16.

IN THE HIGH COURT OF JUSTICE   **1991 E No. 6857**

QUEEN'S BENCH DIVISION

BETWEEN: EYESORE PROPERTY LIMITED   <u>Plaintiff</u>
                                                  and
                                  JOHN LITTLE   <u>Defendant</u>

DEFENCE

1. Save that it is denied that the Plaintiff is entitled to possession
    of the premises, Paragraph 1 of the Statement of Claim is
    admitted.

2. Paragraphs 2 to 5 of the Statement of Claim are admitted.

3. Paragraph 6 of the Statement of Claim is denied. On the 3rd
    January 1991, the Defendant paid the rent for the Christmas
    1990 quarter (£2,500) to John Fortesque & Co., the Plaintiff's
    managing agents in respect of the premises; the money was
    paid in cash and a receipt given for the money.

4. In respect of the rent due on the 25th March and the 24th June
    1991, the Defendant tendered £2,500 on the 27th March and
    the 29th June 1991 respectively, to the said John Fortesque &
    Co., but the said managing agents refused to accept the same
    on behalf of the Plaintiff, and the Defendant now pays the same
    (namely £5,000) into court.

5. Paragraph 7 of the Statement of Claim is denied.

6. Paragraph 8 of the Statement of Claim is admitted.

7. It is denied that the Plaintiff is entitled to interest as pleaded in
    Paragraph 9 of the Statement of Claim or at all.

8. In the premises, it is denied that the Plaintiff is entitled to the
    relief claimed or any relief.

Served the 15th day of August 1991.

The following points should be noted:

- Paragraph 1 of the Statement of Claim contained one
  innocuous allegation (the plaintiff's title) and one
  controversial one (its entitlement to possession).
  Paragraph 1 of the Defence dealt with this by
  admitting the paragraph with an exception in respect
  of the entitlement to possession.

It is preferable to put the exception first, as in the example:

"Save that it is denied that . . . Paragraph 1 . . . is admitted",

rather than:

68

"Paragraph 1 of the Statement of Claim is admitted save that it is denied that the Plaintiff is entitled to possession of the premises."

This device may be used in other situations, for instance where it is desired to deny the whole paragraph save for a single admission.

- Paragraph 2 of the Defence combines the admissions of Paragraphs 2, 3, 4 and 5 of the Statement of Claim into a single paragraph. The alternative is stylistically clumsy, namely:

2. Paragraph 2 of the Statement of Claim is admitted.
3. Paragraph 3 of the Statement of Claim is admitted.
4. Paragraph 4 of the Statement of Claim is admitted.
5. Paragraph 5 of the Statement of Claim is admitted.

- Paragraphs 3 and 4 of the Defence set out the defendant's case in some detail, so that the plaintiff knows exactly what happened. The reference to a receipt having been given is, strictly speaking, incorrect as it refers to a piece of evidence as to payment. However, there is no harm in pleading it here, and it possibly strengthens the defendant's case psychologically by suggesting that it was ludicrous for the landlord to sue for the December quarter when its own agent gave the defendant a receipt for the money.
- The final paragraph of the Defence deals with the relief sought in the prayer and is a typical way of rounding off a Defence neatly. No general traverse has been pleaded; one is not needed, and all the paragraphs of the Statement of Claim have been dealt with.

The second Defence combines a Counterclaim for damages for disrepair. Although Counterclaims are dealt with in the next chapter, it is convenient to introduce the subject now with an example:

IN THE HIGH COURT OF JUSTICE   **1991 E No. 6857**

QUEEN'S BENCH DIVISION

BETWEEN: EYESORE PROPERTY LIMITED   <u>Plaintiff</u>
                                          and
                                    JOHN LITTLE   <u>Defendant</u>

DEFENCE AND COUNTERCLAIM

DEFENCE

1. Save that it is denied that the Plaintiff is entitled to possession of the premises, Paragraph 1 of the Statement of Claim is admitted.

2. Paragraphs 2 to 5 of the Statement of Claim are admitted.

3. As to Paragraph 6 of the Statement of Claim, it is admitted that the Defendant has not paid the rent as alleged, but denied that the Plaintiff is entitled thereto, by reason of the set-off and counterclaim pleaded below.

4. Paragraph 7 of the Statement of Claim is denied.

5. Paragraph 8 of the Statement of Claim is admitted.

6. Paragraph 9 of the Statement of Claim is denied.

7. The Defendant seeks to set off against the Plaintiff's claim for rent and interest such sums as he is awarded on his counterclaim below in extinction or diminution thereof.

8. It is denied that the Plaintiff is entitled to the relief claimed or any relief.

COUNTERCLAIM

9. By Clause 3 of the said lease, the Plaintiff covenanted to keep the structure of the premises, including the roof, main walls and window frames in good and substantial repair.

10. In breach of the said covenant, the Plaintiff has failed to keep the premises in repair.

PARTICULARS

(i)   Water leaked through a large hole in the roof next to the chimney;

(ii)   The walls needed repointing at first floor level;

(iii) 2 wooden window frames on the first floor level were rotten and water leaked through.

11. The Defendant gave the Plaintiff notice of the said disrepair orally in 2 telephone conversations in about September 1990, and by letters from himself dated the 30th September 1990 and his Solicitors dated the 17th October 1990, but the Plaintiff failed to carry out any repairs, whereupon the Defendant arranged for a firm of builders to carry out the work.

12. By reason of the said breach, the Defendant has suffered loss and damage.

PARTICULARS OF SPECIAL DAMAGE

(i) Cost of carrying out roof repairs, repointing of the walls, and replacement of 2 wooden window frames: £3,500, as per invoice of Whistle & Co., General Builders, dated 21st January, 1991.

(ii) Damage to stock (3 paintings) caused by water leakage — £760.

13. Further, the Defendant claims general damages for annoyance and inconvenience, inter alia through having to place buckets under the leaking roof for 4 weeks.

14. Further, the Defendant is entitled to and claims interest on such damages as he is awarded pursuant to Section 35A of the Supreme Court Act 1981 at such rate and for such period as this Honourable Court shall think fit.

AND the Defendant counterclaims:

1. Damages;

2. Interest thereon under Paragraph 14 hereof, to be assessed.

Served the 16th day of August 1991.

71

Chapter 8

Counterclaims

1. Principles

If a defendant to an action alleges that he has a claim or is entitled to any relief or remedy against the plaintiff in respect of *any* matter (whenever and however arising), he may make a counterclaim in the same proceedings, instead of bringing a separate action (O 15 r 2(1)). If he does so, he must add the counterclaim to his Defence, so that the Defence and Counterclaim is a single pleading.

Order 15 r 1 applies to a counterclaim as if the counterclaim were a separate action and as if the person making the counterclaim (ie the defendant) were the plaintiff, and the person against whom it is made (ie the plaintiff) were a defendant. Order 15 r 1 (which was referred to in Chapter 5) provides that relief in respect of more than one cause of action can be brought in a single action. Thus, if a defendant has two or more separate claims against the plaintiff, he can include them all in his counterclaim. However, the court retains the power to prevent the joinder of causes of action or parties if it feels that it would be more convenient if the matters were dealt with separately (O 15 r 5). For example, if the plaintiff brings an action for possession of land occupied by the defendant, the court would probably not permit the defendant to counterclaim for damages for libel against the plaintiff. Accordingly, a defendant should consider whether his counterclaim is really best dealt with in the same set of proceedings.

If money claims are involved, a counterclaim may be for more or less than the claim, and the court has power to give a judgment for the balance to the appropriate party. A defendant who counterclaims for less than the amount of the claim, and who in effect does not dispute the claim, should always consider making a simultaneous payment into court, to protect his position in relation to costs.

The layout of a Defence and Counterclaim is as follows:

IN THE HIGH COURT OF JUSTICE   **1991 P NO. 4867**

QUEEN'S BENCH DIVISION

BETWEEN: HAROLD PUFFIN   <u>Plaintiff</u>
                                         and
                               J. SWANSONG LIMITED   <u>Defendant</u>

DEFENCE AND COUNTERCLAIM

DEFENCE

1.

2.

3.

COUNTERCLAIM

4.

5.

6.

AND the Defendant Counterclaims:

1.

2.

Served the 5th day of March 1991.

Note the following three points:

- The title of the pleading, Defence *and* Counterclaim, is given at the outset, with the Defence and the Counterclaim given their own separate headings. It is wrong to omit the complete title and start with the title "Defence", leaving it to the reader to discover that a Counterclaim has been added, perhaps a few pages into the pleading.
- As with all composite pleadings, the numbering follows on continuously; it does not re-start at Paragraph 1 with the Counterclaim.

- The prayer is in the same form as in a Statement of Claim, except that it is the defendant who is seeking relief, and he "Counterclaims" rather than "Claims".

2. Counterclaiming against additional parties

Where a counterclaiming defendant alleges that any other person (whether or not a party to the action):

(a) is liable to him along with the plaintiff in respect of the subject-matter of the counterclaim, or

(b) claims against such other person any relief relating to or connected with the original subject-matter of the action,

Order 15 r 3(1) provides that he may join that other person as a party against whom the counterclaim is made.

The court has a discretion to rule that there should be a separate trial of the counterclaim (see O 15 r 5(2)), and has the power to strike out the counterclaim, order that it be tried separately or make any other appropriate order. Accordingly, the defendant should consider carefully, before joining any other party, whether it is really appropriate to have all the matters tried together.

The additional party or parties must be joined into the title of the action, which will then look like this:

IN THE HIGH COURT OF JUSTICE   **1991 P No. 4867**

QUEEN'S BENCH DIVISION

BETWEEN:	HAROLD PUFFIN	<u>Plaintiff</u>
	and	
	J. SWANSONG LIMITED	<u>Defendant</u>
	(By Original Action)	
AND BETWEEN:	J. SWANSONG LIMITED	<u>Plaintiff</u>
	and	
	(1) HAROLD PUFFIN	
	(2) PETER GANDER	<u>Defendants</u>
	(By Counterclaim)	

DEFENCE AND COUNTERCLAIM

This may sometimes be a recipe for complication in relation to the parties. In the Defence, the parties will be referred to as the Plaintiff and the Defendant. However, in the counterclaim, the parties are J. Swansong Limited (called the Plaintiff by Counterclaim), Harold Puffin (the First Defendant by Counterclaim) and Peter Gander (the Second Defendant by Counterclaim). The more parties there are, the more long-winded and possibly confusing their description in the pleadings.

Sometimes in order to simplify matters, the parties are referred to by an abbreviated form of their names (compare the introductory paragraph of the Statement of Claim on page 44). Such a system requires paragraph 1 of the Defence and Counterclaim to set out table of references to the parties as follows:

1. In this pleading, the Plaintiff and First Defendant by Counterclaim will be referred to as "Mr. Puffin";

   the Defendant and Plaintiff by Counterclaim will be referred to as "Swansongs";

   the Second Defendant by Counterclaim will be referred to as "Mr. Gander".

It is naturally particularly important that, if this system is used, it is adhered to consistently throughout the pleading. It is equally important for the sake of clarity that subsequent pleadings use the same references to the parties. It is especially annoying and confusing if the pleading next following reverts to referring to the parties as "Second Defendant by Counterclaim" and so on.

An alternative method is to keep the descriptions of the parties to the original action but, in the counterclaim, to refer to them as "the Plaintiff Harold Puffin", "the Defendant J. Swansong Limited" and "the Second Defendant by Counterclaim Peter Gander".

In each case, a decision has to be made depending on the number of parties, the lengths of their names and so on.

Example

The plaintiff, Joseph Tackey Limited, has sued Doreen Harvey for the price of a sofa sold to her. The Statement of

Claim indorsed on the Writ simply claims the price of goods sold and delivered. She wishes to counterclaim for damages for breach of contract because, shortly after buying the sofa, the springs burst through and injured her when she sat on it. She also wishes to sue the manufacturer, Tumbles Furniture Ltd, for damages for negligence.

IN THE HIGH COURT OF JUSTICE   **1991 J No 4867**

QUEEN'S BENCH DIVISION

BETWEEN: JOSEPH TACKEY LIMITED   <u>Plaintiff</u>
and
DOREEN HARVEY   <u>Defendant</u>
(By Original Action)

AND BETWEEN: DOREEN HARVEY   <u>Plaintiff</u>
and
(1) JOSEPH TACKEY LIMITED
(2) TUMBLES FURNITURE LIMITED   <u>Defendants</u>
(By Counterclaim)

DEFENCE AND COUNTERCLAIM

DEFENCE

1. In this pleading, the Plaintiff will be referred to as "Tackeys"; the Defendant will be referred to as "Mrs. Harvey";

   the Second Defendant by Counterclaim will be referred to as "Tumbles".

2. Tackeys are in business as suppliers of high-class furniture, with premises at 45 Bond Road, Brokerville, Surrey.

3. On or about the 14th April 1991, at their said premises Tackeys agreed to sell to Mrs. Harvey a leather "Luxury Parisian" 3-piece suite, comprising a sofa and 2 armchairs for £4,995.

4. There were implied terms in the said contract that the said suite would be of merchantable quality and reasonably fit for its purpose as domestic furniture.

5. The said suite was delivered to Mrs. Harvey on or about the 19th April 1991.

6. In breach of the said terms, the said sofa was neither of merchantable quality, nor fit for its purpose.

PARTICULARS

On the 20th May 1991, when Mrs. Harvey sat on the said sofa, 3 sharp metal springs protruded from the seat and injured her.

7. On the 1st June 1991, Mrs. Harvey telephoned Tackeys' said premises, and spoke to one Hudson, the manager, telling him that she wanted her money back and that they could come and collect the suite. This amounted to rejection of the said suite.

8. In the premises, it is denied that Tackeys are entitled to the sum claimed or any sum.

9. Alternatively, if which is denied, Tackeys are entitled to any sum from Mrs. Harvey, she will seek to set-off such damages as she is awarded under her counterclaim herein in extinction or diminution thereof.

COUNTERCLAIM

10. Mrs. Harvey repeats Paragraphs 1 to 7 of her Defence.

11. By reason of Tackeys' said breach of contract, Mrs. Harvey suffered pain and injury, loss and damage, particulars of which are set out in Paragraph 13 below.

12. Further or alternatively, the injury, loss and damage resulting from the said incident on the 20th May 1991 were caused by the negligence of Tumbles, their servants or agents, who manufactured the said suite and supplied it to Tackeys.

PARTICULARS OF NEGLIGENCE

(i) Failing to secure the springs in the said sofa safely or at all;
(ii) Manufacturing the sofa so that the springs were liable to come through the seat;
(iii) Failing to test the said sofa properly or at all before it left their factory;
(iv) Failing to have proper regard for the safety of persons who would sit on the said sofa.

Mrs. Harvey will rely upon the maxim res ipsa loquitur.

13. By reason of Tumbles' said negligence, Mrs. Harvey suffered pain and injury, loss and damage.

PARTICULARS OF INJURY

(a) Lacerations to the buttocks;
(b) Severance of two nerves in the right thigh;
(c) Consequent permanent scarring to the thigh and buttocks;
(d) Shock.

Mrs. Harvey was born on the 30th May 1952.

PARTICULARS OF SPECIAL DAMAGE

(a) Wasted cost of sofa (if she is liable to pay for it, which is denied).
(b) Cost of replacing slacks damaged beyond repair — £35.

      (c)   Loss of earnings for 6 weeks @ £200 per week —
          £1,200.

      (d)   Taxi fares on 3 round trips to hospital — £45.

14.   Further, Mrs. Harvey claims interest on such damages as she is
awarded pursuant to Section 35A of the Supreme Court Act
1981 at such rate and for such period as this Honourable Court
thinks fit.

AND Mrs. Harvey counterclaims against Tackeys and Tumbles and
each of them:

1.   Damages;

2.   Interest thereon under Paragraph 14, to be assessed.

Served the 18th day of September 1991.

Note the following three points:

- The parties have been referred to by an abbreviated
  form of their names throughout.
- Paragraph 10 of the Counterclaim "repeats" Paragraphs 1 to 7 of the Defence. These paragraphs are
  needed to establish the background leading to the
  claim for damages for breach of contract. For the sake
  of brevity, it is correct to repeat the paragraphs as in
  the example, rather than set them out again.
- The relief pleaded against the defendants is the same,
  namely damages. If the relief sought against
  defendants to a Counterclaim differs, the prayer will
  be divided in the same way as a Statement of Claim
  against two defendants is divided (see page 48).

Chapter 9

Reply and Defence to Counterclaim

1. Reply

Once a Defence has been served, the plaintiff must consider whether it is necessary to serve a Reply. If no Reply is served within 14 days (or any extension of that time limit), pleadings are deemed to be closed (O 18 r 20). Furthermore, by O 18 r 14(1), if no Reply is served, there is an implied joinder of issue on the Defence. This means that all the facts pleaded in the Defence are denied (except for allegations which are specifically admitted in the Defence). Consequently, there is absolutely no point in serving a Reply which simply consists of denials of the Defence; indeed, the costs of such a Reply would probably be disallowed on taxation.

The other side of the coin is that the plaintiff must serve a Reply if he wishes to make a positive allegation in response to a matter raised in the Defence, ie if it is needed to comply with O 18 r 8 (O 18 r 3(1)).

Order 18 r 8(1) provides:

> "A party must in any pleading subsequent to a statement of claim plead specifically any matter, for example, performance, release, the expiry of the relevant period of limitation, fraud or any fact showing illegality –
>
> (a) which he alleges makes any claim or defence of the opposite party not maintainable; or
> (b) which, if not specifically pleaded, might take the opposite party by surprise; or
> (c) which raises issues of fact not arising out of the preceding pleading."

If a Reply is served, it is necessary to deal with every allegation in the Defence, failing which that allegation is deemed to be admitted. Usually, the Reply will be necessary to deal with only part of the Defence (perhaps only one allegation) and, to avoid the danger of unintended admissions, the normal practice is to start the Reply with a paragraph joining issue with the Defence.

A Reply has the same heading as the other pleadings, the title being REPLY.

Example

The plaintiff claims for the price of goods sold and delivered to the defendant. The Defence alleges that the goods were defective and that he is entitled to reject them. The plaintiff wishes to allege that the defendant has accepted the goods under s 35 Sale of Goods Act 1979 because he has kept them for a long time and treated them as his own.

IN THE HIGH COURT OF JUSTICE   **1991 F No. 1234**

QUEEN'S BENCH DIVISION

BETWEEN: FANCY FOOTWORK LIMITED   <u>Plaintiff</u>
                                        and
                    PETER SMITH (trading as LUXURY LOAFERS)
                                                                        <u>Defendant</u>

REPLY

1. Save insofar as it contains admissions, and save as is expressly admitted hereinafter, the Plaintiff joins issue with the Defence.

2. As to Paragraph 3 of the Defence, it is admitted that the shoes were delivered to the Defendant on the 1st February 1991. The Defendant has kept the shoes at his premises at 150 High Street, London E1 ever since, and has stuck his own trading labels on the boxes of each one. The Defendant did not purport to reject the shoes until the 1st September 1991, when he wrote a letter to the Plaintiff. Accordingly, by virtue of Section 35 of the Sale of Goods Act 1979, the Defendant is deemed to have accepted the shoes.

                                                        (Signature)

Served the 15th day of November 1991 by Muggins & Co., Solicitors for the Plaintiff.

It will be seen that Paragraph 1 is rather ungainly and archaic. There are numerous variations on this form of words which do the required job. Strictly speaking, no reference to admissions need be made since one cannot join issue with an admission. It is probably necessary only to say: "The Plaintiff joins issue with the Defence."

If there is more than one defendant and more than one Defence, the Reply must make it clear in the heading and in the body of the pleading which one is being answered:

IN THE HIGH COURT OF JUSTICE   **1991 F No. 1234**

QUEEN'S BENCH DIVISION

BETWEEN: FANCY FOOTWORK LIMITED   <u>Plaintiff</u>

and

PETER SMITH (trading as LUXURY LOAFERS)

<u>First Defendant</u>

and

HARRY JONES   <u>Second Defendant</u>

REPLY TO DEFENCE OF SECOND DEFENDANT

1. The Plaintiff joins issue with the Defence of the Second Defendant.

2. Defence to Counterclaim

If the plaintiff wishes to defend a Counterclaim, he must serve a Defence to it (O 18 r 3(2)). If it is intended to serve a Reply to the Defence and a Defence to the Counterclaim, both must be included in the same document, which is called a Reply and Defence to Counterclaim.

The format is as follows:

IN THE HIGH COURT OF JUSTICE   **1991 F No. 1234**

QUEEN'S BENCH DIVISION

BETWEEN: FANCY FOOTWORK LIMITED   <u>Plaintiff</u>

and

PETER SMITH (trading as LUXURY LOAFERS)

<u>Defendant</u>

REPLY AND DEFENCE TO COUNTERCLAIM

REPLY

1 . . .

2 . . .

3 . . .

DEFENCE TO COUNTERCLAIM

4 . . .

5 . . .

6 . . .

Served . . .

Note that, as with all composite pleadings, (i) the two parts are divided by separate headings and (ii) the paragraph numbers for the body of the pleading follow on continuously; they do not re-start with the Defence to Counterclaim.

If no Reply is needed, because it is intended simply to deny the Defence (see the beginning of this chapter), only a Defence to Counterclaim will be served, which looks like this:

IN THE HIGH COURT OF JUSTICE   1991 F No. 1234

QUEEN'S BENCH DIVISION

BETWEEN: FANCY FOOTWORK LIMITED   <u>Plaintiff</u>

and

PETER SMITH (trading as LUXURY LOAFERS)

<u>Defendant</u>

DEFENCE TO COUNTERCLAIM

1 . . .

2 . . .

3 . . .

Served . . .

Since a Counterclaim is treated as a separate action by the defendant against the plaintiff, the Defence to the Counterclaim is pleaded in the same way as a Defence to a Statement of Claim.

3. Subsequent pleadings

No pleading subsequent to a Reply or a Defence to Counterclaim may be served except with the court's leave (O 18 r 4).

It does not happen very often that a party wishes or needs to serve a further pleading. Occasionally, it will be necessary to serve a Reply to the Defence to Counterclaim, or even a Counterclaim to the Defendant's Counterclaim.

The pleadings subsequent to a Reply are called:

- Rejoinder by Defendant;
- Surrejoinder by Plaintiff;
- Rebutter by Defendant;
- Surrebutter by Plaintiff.

One fairly recent case in which these subsequent pleadings were used was *Tito* v *Waddell (No 2)* [1977] Ch 106, where the judgment refers (at page 124) to an Amended Surrejoinder.

Chapter 10

County court pleadings

1. Particulars of Claim

The system of pleadings in the county courts is, essentially, the same as that in the High Court. In actions begun by plaint, the first pleading is called Particulars of Claim, rather than a Statement of Claim. Otherwise, the names of the pleadings are the same although, curiously, the County Court Rules make no mention of a Reply or indeed any pleading other than Particulars of Claim, Defence, and Counterclaim.

Note that matters begun by originating application do not involve pleadings and are not within the scope of this book.

The layout of Particulars of Claim is as follows:

IN THE PUTWORTH COUNTY COURT   Case No. 9123456

BETWEEN: JOHN O'GRIEF   Plaintiff

and

STRONGHOLD BANK PLC   Defendant

PARTICULARS OF CLAIM

1 . . .

2 . . .

3 . . .

AND the Plaintiff claims:

1 . . .

2 . . .

PETER JONES

Dated the 25th day of May 1991.

Noggins & Co. Solicitors for the Plaintiff
of 32 High Street, London SW18,
where they will accept service of
proceedings on behalf of the Plaintiff.

To the Registrar of the
Putworth County Court and
to the Defendant.

Comparisons may be made with a Statement of Claim in the High Court:

- The case number in the top right hand corner consists only of figures, the first two of which are the last two digits of the year of issue of the proceedings.
- If counsel drafts the pleading, his name must appear on the copy (CCR O 50 r 7).
- The Particulars of Claim must be signed by the Plaintiff if he sues in person, or, if he sues by solicitor, by the solicitor in his own or his firm's name. The Particulars of Claim must state the plaintiff's address for service (CCR O 6 r 8).
- The date of the pleading is given after the word "Dated", rather than "Served".

Subject to one exception, the plaintiff files his Particulars of Claim when commencing the action. The Particulars of Claim must specify his cause of action, the relief or remedy sought, and must state briefly the material facts on which he relies (CCR O 6 r 1(1)).

The exception is where, in an action for debt, the Particulars of Claim can conveniently be incorporated in the form of request for the issue of the summons, and the proper officer of the county court allows this to be done (CCR O 6 r 9(2)). The relevant prescribed forms contain a box for the claim to be set out. This exception does not, of course, avoid the need for clarity and precision in the drafting of the claim.

(a) Value of unliquidated claim

In the case of proceedings started since 1 July 1991, the previous jurisdiction limits applicable to county courts have been fundamentally changed and enlarged. By CCR O 21 r 5,

85

the District Judge (formerly called the registrar) now has jurisdiction to hear any action or matter where the value does not exceed £5,000. In relation to a claim for an unliquidated sum, the value of the plaintiff's claim for the purposes of CCR O 21 r 5(1) will be treated as being limited to £5,000, unless (a) the plaintiff states in his Particulars of Claim or otherwise that the value of his claim exceeds the said sum; or (b) the court orders otherwise (CCR O 6 r 1(1A)). Furthermore, where a statement is made under (a), the plaintiff must forthwith file an amended statement whenever the value of his claim falls to £5,000 or less.

It is suggested that the best way of complying with this provision is to include it in the prayer, for example as follows:

AND the Plaintiff claims:

1. Damages (which exceed £5,000);
2. . . . .

(b) Excessive claim

If the plaintiff claims more than the county court has jurisdiction to award, he may abandon the excess in order to give the county court jurisdiction (s 17 County Courts Act 1984). In that case, the abandonment must be stated at the end of the Particulars (CCR O 6 r 1(3)) thus:

The Plaintiff abandons his claim for damages insofar as it exceeds £5,000 [ie the county court limit before 1 July 1991].

(c) Interest

As in the High Court, a claim for interest must be pleaded (CCR O 6 r 1A). This rule applies whether the claim is under s 69 County Courts Act 1984 (the equivalent to s 35A Supreme Court Act 1981), or otherwise.

(d) Damages

Where a plaintiff claims:

    (i) aggravated damages;
    (ii) exemplary damages, or
    (iii) provisional damages,

his Particulars of Claim must contain a statement to that effect and must state the facts on which he relies in support of his claim for such damages (CCR O 6 r 1(B)).

2. Requirements for specific types of action

Six types of action have particular requirements in CCR O 6 and are dealt with in turn.

(a) Personal injuries

As in the High Court, the plaintiff must now file with his Particulars of Claim (i) a medical report and (ii) a statement of the special damages claimed, together with a copy of those documents for each defendant (CCR O 6 r 1 (5)).

This does not absolve the plaintiff from pleading details in the Particulars of Claim.

"Medical report" means a report substantiating all the personal injuries alleged in the Particulars of Claim which the plaintiff proposes to adduce in evidence as part of his case at the trial.

"A statement of the special damages claimed" means a statement giving full particulars of the special damages claimed for expenses and losses already incurred and an estimate of any future expenses and losses (including loss of earnings and of pension rights).

If these documents are not filed with the Particulars of Claim, the court may (i) specify a period of time within which they are to be provided, in which case the plaintiff must comply with the time limit; or (ii) make such other order as it thinks fit, including dispensing with the requirements to serve the documents, or staying the proceedings.

(b) Claim for an account

Where the plaintiff wishes to have an account taken, the Particulars of Claim must contain a statement to that effect, and must specify the amount which he claims, subject to the taking of the account. If no amount is stated, the plaintiff is deemed to claim the maximum sum which may be recovered in the action (CCR O 6 r 2).

Until 1 July 1991, the maximum amount claimable depended upon the county court jurisdiction limit appropriate to the nature of the claim. Accordingly, if the claim for an account was made in breach of contract proceedings, the plaintiff was limited to payment of £5,000.

(c) Recovery of land

CCR O 6 r 3(1) sets out what must be stated in the Particulars of Claim in an action for recovery of land:

(i) the land sought to be recovered;
(ii) the net annual value for rating of the land or, if the land does not consist of one or more hereditaments having at the time when the action is commenced a separate net annual value for rating:

- the net annual value of that hereditament, or
- the value of the land by the year (ie the yearly market rental value).

CCR O 6 r 3(3) provides that in relation to domestic property (within the meaning of s 66 Local Government Finance Act 1988), references to the net annual value for rating or the net value for rating are to be construed as references to the value shown on the valuation list on 31 March 1990, or to its value by the year, as the case may be − this is a consequence of the abolition of domestic rates on that date;

(iii) the rent, if any, of the land;
(iv) the ground on which possession is claimed;
(v) in a case to which s 138 County Courts Act 1984 applies (ie a case of forfeiture for non-payment of rent), the daily rate at which the rent in arrear is to be calculated;
(vi) in proceedings for forfeiture where the plaintiff knows of any person entitled to claim relief against forfeiture as underlessee (including a mortgagee) under s 146(4) Law of Property Act 1925 or under s 138(9C) County Courts Act 1984, the name and address of that person. In such a case, the plaintiff

must file a copy of the Particulars of Claim for service on the person named (CCR O 6 r 3(2)).

Example

The plaintiff wishes to claim possession of a residential house by forfeiting the lease for non-payment of rent. The lease created a protected tenancy under the Rent Act 1977. The plaintiff knows there is a sub-tenant of part of the premises.

IN THE KEWSBURY COUNTY COURT　　　　**Case no. 9134567**

BETWEEN:　　　　　　　JASON FLEECE　　　　　.　Plaintiff
　　　　　　　　　　　　　　and
　　　　　　　　　　MARJORIE MINK　　　　　Defendant

PARTICULARS OF CLAIM

1. The Plaintiff is the freehold owner and entitled to possession of the premises known as 123 Acacia Avenue, London NW8, hereinafter called "the premises".

2. By a tenancy agreement dated the 15th June 1987, the Plaintiff let the premises to the Defendant for a term of 5 years at a rent of £2,000 per annum, payable quarterly in advance on the usual quarter days.

3. Clause 4 of the said agreement contained a proviso for re-entry in the event, inter alia, that the said rent should be in arrears for 14 days after falling due.

4. In breach of the said agreement, the Defendant has failed to pay the rent for the quarters due on the June 1990, September 1990, December 1990 and March 1991 and is thus £2,500 in arrears, and the said agreement has become forfeited to the Plaintiff.

5. The Defendant is a statutory tenant of the premises and possession is claimed pursuant to Case 1 of Schedule 15 to the Rent Act 1977.

6. On the 31st March 1990, the net annual value for rating of the premises was £405.

7. The said rent is equivalent to a daily rate of £6.85.

8. One Peter Jones is a sub-tenant of part of the premises, residing at that address, and is entitled to claim relief from forfeiture.

9. Further, the Plaintiff is entitled to and claims interest on the said arrears of rent under Section 69 of the County Courts Act 1984

@ 15% per annum, amounting to £[insert figure] to the date hereof, and continuing at the daily rate of £1.03 until judgment or sooner payment.

AND the Plaintiff claims:

1. Possession of the premises;
2. Arrears of rent of £2,500 to the date hereof;
3. Interest thereon amounting to £[insert figure] to the date hereof, and continuing at the daily rate of £1.03 until judgment or sooner payment.
4. Rent/mesne profits @ £2,500 per annum, equal to a daily rate of £6.85 from the 24th June 1991 until possession is delivered up. [N.B. The claim for rent, being payable in advance, goes up to the June 1991 quarter day.]

Dated the 16th April 1991.

(d) Injunction or declaration relating to land

Where the plaintiff claims an injunction or declaration in respect of, or in relation to, any land, or the possession, occupation, use or enjoyment of any land, the Particulars of Claim must contain the information set out in CCR O 6 r 3(1)(a) (the land sought to be recovered) and in CCR O 6 r 3(1)(b) (the rateable value etc): see page 88 in relation to claims for the recovery of land.

(e) Mortgage action

By CCR O 6 r 5, where a plaintiff claims as mortgagee payment of moneys secured by a mortgage of real or leasehold property or possession of such property, he must in his Particulars of Claim:

(i) state the date of the mortgage;
(ii) show the state of the account between the plaintiff and the defendant with particulars of:

- the amount of the advance,
- the amount of the periodic payments required to be made,
- the amount of any interest or instalments in arrear at the commencement of the proceedings, and
- the amount remaining due under the mortgage;

(iii) state what proceedings, if any, the plaintiff has previously taken against the defendant in respect of the moneys secured by the mortgage or the mortgaged property and, where payment of such moneys only is claimed, whether the plaintiff has obtained possession of the property;

(iv) state, where possession of the property is claimed, whether or not the property consists of or includes a dwelling-house within the meaning of s 21 County Courts Act 1984; and

(v) where he claims as mortgagee possession of land which consists of or includes a dwelling-house, state whether there is any person on whom notice of the action is required to be served in accordance with s 8(3) Matrimonial Homes Act 1983 and, if so, the name and address of that person. In such a case, he must file a copy of the Particulars of Claim for service on that person.

"Mortgage" is defined as including a legal or equitable mortgage and a legal or equitable charge, and references to the mortgaged property and mortgagee are construed accordingly.

Example

A building society wants to claim possession of mortgaged property where the mortgagor has fallen into arrears.

IN THE HINDFORD COUNTY COURT   **Case No. 9178694**

BETWEEN: SUBURB BUILDING SOCIETY   <u>Plaintiff</u>
and
ARTHUR TWEE   <u>Defendant</u>

PARTICULARS OF CLAIM

1. By a Legal Charge dated the 31st August 1986 and made between the Defendant and the Plaintiff, the Defendant mortgaged the land and dwelling-house known as 15 Torrington Place, Hindford, in the County of Surrey (which is a dwelling-house within the meaning of Section 21 of the County Courts Act 1984) to the Plaintiff to secure the repayment by the Defendant to the Plaintiff of the principal sum of £75,000 advanced by the Plaintiff to the Defendant, and interest thereon at the rate of 18% per annum, subject to variation, and

the Defendant covenanted to repay the said principal sum together with interest thereon over the period of 25 years, and covenanted that so long as the principal sum should remain unpaid he would pay to the Plaintiff monthly instalments of £800, subject to variation, in respect of capital and interest.

2. The Defendant failed to pay the instalments due in January, February, March, April, and May 1991, namely £5,134.87, which sum is now in arrears.

3. The amount due under the said Legal Charge at the date hereof is as follows:

Principal — £72,500

Arrears of instalments — £5,134.87

Interest continues at the rate of 19%, and the current monthly instalments are £920.87.

4. The Plaintiff has not previously taken any proceedings against the Defendant in respect of the moneys secured by the said legal charge or the mortgaged property.

5. There is no person on whom notice of the action is required to be served in accordance with Section 8(3) of the Matrimonial Homes Act 1983.

6. The rateable value of the said land and dwelling-house on the 31st March 1990 did not exceed £1,000.

AND the Plaintiff claims possession of the said land and dwelling-house.

Dated the 13th day of June 1991.

(f) Hire purchase actions

CCR Order 6 r 6 sets out what must be contained in the Particulars of Claim in claims arising from hire purchase agreements. Two types of claim are dealt with, and in both, the matters set out in the rule must be stated *in the order* in which they are set out in the rule. The expressions used in this rule have the same definitions as set out in the Consumer Credit Act 1974.

CCR Order 6 r 6(1) sets out what must be contained in the Particulars of Claim *where the plaintiff claims the delivery of goods* let under a hire purchase agreement to a person other than a body corporate, namely:

"(i) the date of the agreement and the parties to it with the number of the agreement or sufficient particulars to enable the debtor to identify the agreement;

   (ii) where the plaintiff was not one of the original parties to the agreement, the means by which the rights and duties of the creditor under the agreement passed to him;

  (iii) whether the agreement is a regulated agreement and, if it is not a regulated agreement, the reason why;

  (iv) the place where the agreement was signed by the debtor (if known);

   (v) the goods claimed;

  (vi) the total price of the goods;

 (vii) the paid-up sum;

(viii) the unpaid balance of the total price;

  (ix) whether a default notice or a notice under section 76(1) or section 98(1) of the Consumer Credit Act 1974 has been served on the debtor, and if it has, the date on which and the manner in which it was so served;

   (x) the date when the right to demand delivery of the goods accrued;

  (xi) the amount (if any) claimed as an alternative to the delivery of the goods;

 (xii) the amount (if any) claimed in addition to the delivery of the goods or any claim under sub-paragraph (xi), stating the cause of action in respect of which each such claim is made."

Example

The following is a sample Particulars of Claim containing the required information. Great care should be exercised in using precedents where (as here) a lot of detailed information is prescribed by the Rules. In one precedent from a very respected source seen by the author, the draftsman has omitted to give a considerable amount of the mandatory information. In another, the Particulars of Claim start as an ordinary pleading, then there is a heading "Particulars under Order 6 r 6(1)" and much of the already pleaded information is repeated. This repetition should obviously be avoided.

IN THE GODALTON COUNTY COURT　　　Case No. 9254678

BETWEEN:　　　　　　GRASPING FINANCE LIMITED　　　<u>Plaintiff</u>
and
FIONA GULLIBLE　　　<u>Defendant</u>

PARTICULARS OF CLAIM

1. By a hire purchase agreement dated the 15th April 1991, made between the Plaintiff and the Defendant numbered GF912345, the Plaintiff let to the Defendant on hire purchase a Sushi video camera and recorder. The Defendant agreed to pay a deposit of £700 and 36 monthly instalments of £100, payable on the 15th of each month.

2. The said agreement is a regulated agreement.

3. The said agreement was signed by the Defendant at 123 High Street, Godalton, Middlesex.

4. The goods claimed are the said video camera and recorder.

5. The total price of the goods was £4,300.

6. In breach of the said agreement, the Defendant made no payments to the Plaintiff after December 1991. The paid-up sum is £1,500.

7. The unpaid balance of the total price is £2,800.

8. A default notice was served on the Defendant by recorded delivery on the 15th March 1992.

9. The right to demand delivery of the said goods accrued on the 23rd March 1992.

10. As an alternative to the delivery of the goods, the Plaintiff claims £3,100.

11. In addition, the Plaintiff claims £300 arrears of instalments.

12. Further, the Plaintiff is entitled to and claims interest on such sums as are found due to him pursuant to Section 69 of the County Courts Act 1984 at such rate and for such period as the court thinks fit.

AND the Plaintiff claims:

1. An order for delivery up of the said video camera and recorder, or £3,100 its value;

2. £300 arrears of instalments;

3. Interest under paragraph 12 hereof to be assessed.

Dated the 4th day of April 1992.

The other type of action covered by CCR O 6 r 6 is where the plaintiff's claim arises out of a hire purchase agreement but is *not for the delivery of goods.*

The Particulars of Claim must contain the following matters in the following order:

"(i) the date of the agreement and the parties to it with the number of the agreement or sufficient particulars to enable the debtor to identify the agreement;

(ii) where the plaintiff was not one of the original parties to the agreement, the means by which the rights and duties of the creditor under the agreement passed to him;

(iii) whether the agreement is a regulated agreement and, if it is not a regulated agreement, the reason why;

(iv) the place where the agreement was signed by the debtor (if known);

(v) the goods let under the agreement;

(vi) the amount of the total price;

(vii) the paid-up sum;

(viii) the amount (if any) claimed as being due and unpaid in respect of any instalment or instalments of the total price; and

(ix) the nature and amount of any other claim and the circumstances in which it arises."

As with the example given above, the Particulars of Claim must contain all this information in the right order, appropriately fleshed out in pleading form.

The rules for pleading a Defence and Further and Better Particulars are essentially the same as in the High Court.

Chapter 11

Third Party Notices

1. High Court

The procedure for a defendant bringing a third party into the proceedings is dealt with by RSC O 16. He does so by serving a Third Party Notice.

If the Third Party Notice is not sufficiently detailed, directions may be given for the defendant to serve a Statement of Claim on the Third Party, and subsequent pleadings will follow. It should be remembered that a Third Party Notice is not equivalent to a Statement of Claim requiring a Defence to be served pending directions from the court.

In three cases, a Third Party Notice may be issued by a defendant who has given Notice of Intention to Defend:

    (i) where he claims against a person not already a party any contribution or indemnity; or

    (ii) where he claims against such a person any relief or remedy relating to or connected with the original subject-matter of the action and substantially the same as some other relief or remedy claimed by the plaintiff; or

    (iii) where the defendant requires that any question or issue relating to or connected with the original subject-matter of the action should be determined not only as between the plaintiff and the defendant but also as between either or both of them and a person not already a party to the action.

Typical situations giving rise to a Third Party Notice include the following:

- the original lessee is sued by the lessor for arrears of rent which have accrued since he assigned the lease. He can make the assignee a third party, seeking an indemnity (as in the first example below);
- a person who has caused a road accident is sued. He wishes to claim a contribution from another driver who he alleges contributed to the accident;
- only one guarantor of a contract is sued. He can serve a Third Party Notice on the other guarantors.

There are two prescribed forms of Third Party Notice, one for use in claims (i) or (ii) above, and the other for (iii). The defendant requires leave to issue a Third Party Notice unless it is issued before the Defence is served. If leave is granted, the order is referred to in the Notice.

Examples

Third Party Notice claiming contribution or indemnity or other relief or remedy:

IN THE HIGH COURT OF JUSTICE   **1991 S No. 8993**

QUEEN'S BENCH DIVISION

BETWEEN: JEREMIAH SMITH   <u>Plaintiff</u>
and
CATHERINE CURMUDGEON   <u>Defendant</u>
and
CHRISTOPHER CHOLIC   <u>Third Party</u>

THIRD PARTY NOTICE

Issued pursuant to the order of Master Plan dated the 16th day of October 1991.

To Christopher Cholic of 65 Laburnum Avenue, Wickham, in the County of Somerset.

Take Notice that this action has been brought by the Plaintiff against the Defendant. In it the Plaintiff claims against the Defendant arrears of rent and interest as appears from the Writ of Summons a copy whereof is served herewith together with a copy of the Statement of Claim.

The Defendant claims against you to be indemnified against the Plaintiff's claim and the costs of this action on the grounds that:

(1)   The Defendant assigned the residue of the term of the lease referred to in the Statement of Claim to you on the 13th December 1985.

(2) In the Deed of Assignment you covenanted to pay the rent to the landlord and keep the Defendant indemnified against any claims arising under the said lease.

(3) If, which is not admitted, the rent has not been paid by you to the Plaintiff as alleged in the Statement of Claim, you are accordingly liable to indemnify the Defendant under the said covenant.

AND TAKE NOTICE that within 14 days after service of this Notice on you, counting the day of service, you must acknowledge service and state in your acknowledgement whether you intend to contest the proceedings. If you fail to do so, or if your acknowledgement does not state your intention to contest the proceedings, you will be deemed to admit the Plaintiff's claim against the Defendant and the Defendant's claim against you and your liability to indemnify the Defendant and will be bound by any judgment or decision given in the action, and the judgment may be enforced against you in accordance with Order 16 of the Rules of the Supreme Court 1965.

Dated the 3rd day of October 1991.

Noggins

Solicitors for the Defendant

IMPORTANT

Directions for acknowledgement of service are given with the accompanying form.

Third Party Notice where question or issue to be determined:

IN THE HIGH COURT OF JUSTICE   **1991 S No. 8993**

QUEEN'S BENCH DIVISION

BETWEEN: JEREMIAH SMITH   <u>Plaintiff</u>
                                         and
                      CATHERINE CURMUDGEON   <u>Defendant</u>
                                         and
                      CHRISTOPHER CHOLIC   <u>Third Party</u>

THIRD PARTY NOTICE

Issued pursuant to the order of Master Plan dated the 16th day of October 1991.

To Christopher Cholic of 65 Laburnum Avenue, Wickham, in the County of Somerset.

Take Notice that this action has been brought by the Plaintiff against the Defendant. In it the Plaintiff claims against the Defendant arrears of rent and interest as appears from the Writ of Summons a copy whereof is served herewith together with a copy of the Statement of Claim.

The Defendant requires that following question or issue, viz., an agreement dated the 23rd April 1988 made between the Plaintiff, the Defendant and you is void for illegality should be determined not only as between the Plaintiff and the Defendant but also as between either or both of them and yourself.

AND TAKE NOTICE that within 14 days after service of this Notice on you, counting the day of service, you must acknowledge service and state in your acknowledgement whether you intend to contest the proceedings. If you fail to do so, or if your acknowledgement does not state your intention to contest the proceedings, you will be bound by any judgment or decision in the action so far as it is relevant to the said question or issue, and the judgment may be enforced against you in accordance with Order 16 of the Rules of the Supreme Court 1965.

Dated the 3rd day of October 1991.

Noggins
Solicitors for the Defendant

IMPORTANT

Directions for acknowledgement of service are given with the accompanying form.

2. County court

The equivalent procedure in the county court is set out in CCR O 12. The form of Third Party Notice to be used is N.15, an example of which is as follows:

IN THE WIMBLEWORTH COUNTY COURT   **Case No. 9244567**

BETWEEN: HAVABASH LIMITED   Plaintiff
                        and
                G.H. BARLOW (FEMALE)   Defendant
                        and
        JEREMY FLOATER (trading as SINKINGS)   Third Party

To Jeremy Floater

TAKE NOTICE that this action has been brought by the Plaintiff against the Defendant and that the Defendant claims against you

(a) that he is entitled to contribution from you to the extent of . . .

   or

(b) that he is entitled to be indemnified by you against liability in respect of . . .

   or

(c) that he is entitled to the following relief or remedy relating to or connected with the original subject matter of the action, namely . . .

or

(d) that the following question or issue relating to or connected with the subject matter of the action should properly be determined as between the Plaintiff and the Defendant and the Third Party, namely . . .

The grounds of the Defendant's claim are - . . .

If you dispute the Plaintiff's claim against the Defendant or the Defendant's claim against you, you must within 14 days after service of this notice upon you take or send to the court two copies of your defence.

AND TAKE NOTICE that you should attend at the Wimbleworth County Court, Upper Richmond Road, London SW15 on the 13th October 1992 at 10.30 a.m. when directions will be given for the further conduct of these proceedings.

If you fail to attend you may be deemed to admit:

(1) the Plaintiff's claim against the Defendant; and

(2) the Defendant's claim against you; and

(3) your liability to (contribute to the extent claimed) or (indemnify the Defendant); or

(4) the Defendant's right to the relief or remedy claimed in paragraph (c) above; and

(5) the validity of any judgment in the action;

And you will be bound by the judgment in the action.

Dated the 1st day of September 1991.

Chapter 12

Amendment of pleadings

It is hardly surprising that in many cases, between the time the original Writ is issued and the final hearing, at least one party wishes to amend the pleadings. As we have seen, the court can make decisions only on the basis of the pleadings. A party's case may well change over time; allegations will be abandoned, new evidence comes to light, a fresh mind is brought to bear on the case. Provided the other party can be compensated in costs, and is not prejudiced, the court will allow the amendment; this is because it is in the interests of justice that the real dispute between the parties is decided, even though their pleadings were not originally fully or properly drafted.

The rules as to the amendment of Writs and pleadings are set out in RSC O 20. As will be seen, in some cases amendments may be made without the leave of the court; in others, leave must be obtained. It is necessary to carry out a brief review of the rules before seeing how amendments are made.

1. Amendments without leave

(a) Writ

In general, the plaintiff may, without the leave of the court, amend the Writ once at any time before the pleadings in the action begun by the Writ are closed (O 20 r 1(1)).

This is subject to exceptions, namely where the amendment consists of:

    (i) the addition, omission or substitution of a party to the action or the alteration of the capacity in which a party to the action sues or is sued; or

(ii) the addition or substitution of a new cause of action; or

(iii) (without prejudice to r 3(1)) an amendment of the Statement of Claim (if any) indorsed on the Writ.

Order 20 r 3(1) permits a party, without leave, to amend any pleading once before pleadings are deemed to be closed. These exceptions do not apply if the amendment is made before service of the Writ on any party to the action; before the Writ has been served, it may be amended in any way at all.

(b) Pleadings

We have seen above that a party may amend any pleading once without leave before the close of pleadings.

Where an amended Statement of Claim is served on a defendant, the defendant, if he has already served a Defence on the plaintiff, may amend his Defence, and has 14 days from service of the amended Statement of Claim to serve his original or amended Defence.

Where an amended Defence is served, the plaintiff may amend his reply; he has a further 14 days, as for an amended Defence. The same principles apply to a Counterclaim and Defence to Counterclaim.

If a party is faced with an amended pleading and has already pleaded to the original, he does not have to amend his pleading in reply. If he does not do so, he is deemed to have joined issue on all the allegations made by the amendments.

(c) Disallowance of amendments (O 20 r 4)

Within 14 days after service on a party of an amended Writ or pleading made without leave, that party may apply to the court to disallow the amendment. Any order made on such an application may be on such terms as to costs or otherwise as the court thinks just.

Where the court hearing the application is satisfied that, if an application for leave to make the amendment in question had been made under O 20 r 5 at the date when the amendment was made, leave to make the amendment or part

102

of the amendment would have been refused, it will order the amendment or that part to be struck out.

Order 20 r 5 is discussed below. An example of an amendment that would be disallowed is an amendment to a Statement of Claim, whether or not indorsed on the Writ, to add a cause of action accruing to the plaintiff after the issue of the Writ. Thus, if the plaintiff gives a notice to the defendant expiring after the Writ was issued, a cause of action depending on expiry of the notice cannot be added to the proceedings begun by the Writ; it would be necessary to commence fresh proceedings.

2. Amendments with leave

The power to amend the Writ or pleadings with leave is contained in O 20 r 5. By r 5(1), subject to O 15 rr 6, 7 and 8 (see below) and the following provisions of r 5, the court may at any stage of the proceedings allow the plaintiff to amend his Writ, or any party to amend his pleadings, on such terms as to costs or otherwise as may be just and in such manner (if any) as it may direct.

There is no restriction on the number of times the Writ or pleadings may be amended with leave. In addition, O 20 r 8 provides a general power to amend any document in the proceedings (other than judgments or orders) for the purpose of determining the real question in controversy between the parties, or of correcting any defect or error in the proceedings. The court may act at any stage of the proceedings either of its own motion, or on the application of a party, and may impose any terms it thinks just.

Order 15 rr 6, 7 and 8 deal with the misjoinder and nonjoinder of parties, the change of parties caused by death or bankruptcy, and consequential matters.

The remaining provisions of r 5 deal with specific types of amendment. By r 5(2), where an application to the court for leave to make the amendments mentioned in paragraphs (3), (4) or (5) is made after any relevant period of limitation current at the date of issue of the Writ has expired, the court may nevertheless grant such leave in the circumstances mentioned in that paragraph if it thinks it just to do so. "Any relevant period of limitation" includes a time limit which applies to the proceedings in question by virtue of the Foreign Limitation Periods Act 1984.

(i) Amendment of name (O 20 r 5(3))

An amendment to correct the name of a party may be allowed under paragraph (2) notwithstanding that it is alleged that the effect of the amendment will be to substitute a new party if the court is satisfied that the mistake sought to be corrected was a genuine mistake and was not misleading or such as to cause any reasonable doubt as to the identity of the person intending to sue or, as the case may be, intended to be sued.

(ii) Amendment of capacity (O 20 r 5(4))

An amendment to alter the capacity in which a party sues may be allowed under paragraph (2) if the new capacity is one which that party had at the date of the commencement of the proceedings or has since acquired.

(iii) Amendment of cause of action (O 20 r 5(5))

An amendment may be allowed under paragraph (2) notwithstanding that the effect of the amendment will be to add or substitute a new cause of action if the new cause of action arises out of the same facts or substantially the same facts as a cause of action in respect of which relief has already been claimed in the action by the party applying for leave to make the amendment.

(iv) Retrospective nature of amendment

An amendment takes effect from the date of the original document. It is this important rule which is the reason why, for instance, the Writ may not be amended to add a cause of action which has accrued since the date it was issued, and why the court will be bound to give careful consideration to any amendment possibly affecting the limitation position, eg the potentially difficult question of depriving a party of an accrued right to rely on a limitation defence. For a detailed discussion of the limitation problem, see *The Supreme Court Practice* (1991) paras 20/5 – 8/7 – 8/8.

(v) Time for amending

Amendments may be allowed at any stage of the proceedings – this includes before, at or after the trial, exceptionally even after judgment or on appeal. However, since the power to allow amendments is discretionary, the later the application is made, the less likely it is to be granted. This is because the other party is more likely to be prejudiced, and not able to be fully protected by an order for costs.

3. Method of making amendments

(a) Indorsement

An amended Writ or pleading must be indorsed with a statement that it has been amended, specifying:

- (i) the date on which it was amended,
- (ii) the name of the judge, master or district judge by whom the order (if any) authorising the amendment was made and the date thereof, or
- (iii) if no such order was made, the number of the rule of O 20 in pursuance of which the amendment was made.

Examples

When amendment made without leave:
At top of pleading:

Amended without leave pursuant to Order 20 rule 3 of the Rules of the Supreme Court

At end:

Served the 15th day of April 1991
Re-served the 30th day of July 1991

When amendment made with leave:
At top of pleading:

Amended pursuant to the Order of Master Gubbins dated the 25th July 1991

At end:

Served the 15th day of April 1991
Re-served the 30th day of July 1991

(b) Form of amendment

This depends on whether or not the amendments are brief. If they are brief, the original document may be altered, by deleting and inserting words as appropriate. If the amendments are so numerous or of such nature or length that to make written alterations would make it difficult or inconvenient to read, a fresh document must be prepared and, in the case of a Writ or Originating Summons, reissued.

In the case of a Writ, the original will be resealed with the words:

Superseded by amendment

and the amended Writ indorsed with the words:

Reissued on amendment

In the case of a pleading, the amended pleading is indorsed with the words:

Replaced by Amendment made the 14th day of May 1991, under RSC Order 20 rule 3

if leave was not required, or

Replaced by amendment made the 14th day of May 1991, pursuant to order dated the 14th day of May 1991

if leave was required.

For the practice on resealing the Writ, whether or not indorsed with a Statement of Claim, see *The Supreme Court Practice* (1991) paras 20/1/6 and 20/3–4/2.

By *Masters' Practice Direction 20*, amendments must be made in different coloured inks:

- a first amendment must be in red;
- a second, or re-amendment, must be in green;
- a third, or re-re-amendment, must be in violet;
- a fourth, or re-re-re-amendment, must be in yellow.

Any further amendments must be in colours ordered by the court when leave is given.

The names of amended pleadings are Amended Statement of Claim, Re-amended Statement of Claim, Re-re-amended Statement of Claim etc.

The amendment is made by deleting and adding any appropriate words in the correct colour. The deletion should be by way of a thin straight line through the old word, leaving the word deleted still legible, if possible. The old word should not be completely obliterated. Where new words are added, they may either be written in the correct coloured ink, or (more commonly) written in black and underlined in the correct coloured ink.

It is very important to note that the whole of the original pleading must be contained in the amendment, duly deleted where necessary. It is not correct simply to omit a paragraph which is not relied upon. The other parties and the court must be able to see from the latest pleading the full nature of all the amendments.

In the case of *Re Langton, Langton* v *Lloyds Bank Ltd* [1960] 1 WLR 246, it was held that the party (in that case, a plaintiff acting in person) could amend his Statement of Claim once without leave in any colour. However, to avoid confusion, it is good practice to follow the usual colour guide, even if the amendment is made without leave.

Chapter 13

Drafting affidavits

As with pleadings, in drafting affidavits it is necessary to comply with the relevant rules, as well as using an appropriate style. The correct style for affidavits is, however, markedly different from that used in pleadings. An affidavit is a sworn statement from a witness, known as a "deponent". Particularly in the case of a lay deponent, it is important to avoid using language which the witness is unable to understand. Remember that he may be cross-examined upon the contents of the affidavit. It is not unknown for a witness to say that he does not understand his own affidavit, which was drafted for him by his solicitor and sworn by him on trust. For obvious reasons this is highly undesirable.

1. Formalities

RSC Order 41 sets out the rules for affidavits. By CCR O 20 r 10, most of the same rules apply in the county court (see the section below on county courts).

(a) Binding

Affidavits must not be bound with thick plastic strips or anything else which would hamper filing.

(b) Title

The basic rule is that the affidavit is entitled in the same way as the pleadings in the cause or matter in which it is sworn. However, in the following cases, an abbreviated title may be used:

(i) Where a cause or matter is entitled in more than one matter, it is sufficient to state the first matter, followed by "and other matters".

(ii) Where a cause or matter is entitled in a matter or matters and between parties, that part of the title which consists of the matter or matters may be omitted.

(iii) Where there is more than one plaintiff and/or defendant, only the first need be stated in full, followed by "and others".

(c) Marking

In order to assist in finding the appropriate affidavit out of a large bundle of documents, since 1983 all affidavits in the High Court must have written in clear permanent blue or black marking in the top right hand corner of the first page (and also on the back sheet) the following information:

(i) the party on whose behalf it is filed;

(ii) the initials and surname of the deponent;

(iii) the number of the affidavit in relation to the deponent;

(iv) the date when sworn.

Example

1st Dft: W.S. Gilbert: 2nd: 1.4.91

This indicates the second affidavit of W.S. Gilbert, sworn on behalf of the First Defendant, on the 1st April 1991.

Despite the fact that this rule has been in force for several years, many affidavits still omit the required marking, causing endless annoyance to judges, masters and district judges.

(d) Commencement

Every affidavit must be expressed in the first person.

Unless the court otherwise directs, it must state the place of residence of the deponent and his occupation or, if he has none, his description, and if he is, or is employed by, a party to the cause or matter in which the affidavit is sworn, the affidavit must state that fact.

In the case of a deponent who is giving evidence in a professional, business or other occupational capacity the affidavit may, instead of stating the deponent's place of residence, state the address at which he works, the position he holds and the name of his firm or employer, if any.

The following is the usual form:

> I, William Shakespeare, of Hathaway Cottage, 9 Hamlet Street, Stratford-upon-Avon, Warwickshire, actor, make oath and say as follows:

If the deponent does not wish to swear the affidavit on oath, he may affirm, in which case the document is called an Affirmation. The commencing words then read:

> I, William Shakespeare, of Hathaway Cottage, 9 Hamlet Street, Stratford-upon-Avon, Warwickshire, actor, do solemnly and sincerely affirm:

(e) Body

The text of the affidavit must be divided into paragraphs numbered consecutively.

Each paragraph must, as far as possible, be confined to a distinct portion of the subject.

Dates, sums and other numbers must be expressed in an affidavit in figures and not in words.

If the deponent is one of the parties, he should say so in the body of the pleading (even though this may appear obvious from his name). The way of referring to this is to start the affidavit:

> 1.   I am the above-named Second Plaintiff . . .

If the deponent is not a party, he should state that he is authorised to make the affidavit on behalf of the person or party in question, as follows:

> 1.   I am duly authorised to make this affidavit on behalf of the Plaintiff . . .

If the deponent is giving his expert opinion on a topic in the affidavit, the first paragraph should set out the academic qualifications and experience which entitle him to be regarded as an expert witness.

Subject to the following exceptions, an affidavit may contain only such facts as the deponent is able of his own knowledge to prove. If it is not clear from the context, the affidavit ought to state how the deponent acquired his knowledge of the facts. The exceptions are:

   (i) an affidavit sworn for the purpose of being used in interlocutory proceedings may contain statements of information or belief with the sources and grounds thereof;

  (ii) an affidavit for use in an application for summary judgment under O 14 or specific performance under O 86 may contain statements of information or belief with the sources and grounds thereof;

 (iii) under O 38 r 3, the court may order that evidence of any fact may be given at the trial by statement on oath of information or belief;

 (iv) under O 113 r 3, an affidavit in support of an application for summary possession of land (a squatter's action), may contain statements of information or belief with the sources and grounds thereof.

In such a case, the affidavit could read:

> I am informed by my employer John Smith and believe that on the 15th July 1990 he saw the Defendant damage my car by hitting it with a hammer.

Traditionally, the statement of belief has included the word "verily", ie "I am informed by ... and verily believe that ...". This is archaic and should not be used; it is not required by the rules. No less a figure than Staughton LJ has recently written a number of articles deploring the continued use of such old-fashioned language.

An affidavit may not contain any matter which is scandalous, irrelevant or otherwise oppressive. Any such material may be struck out by the court under O 41 r 6.

Affidavits should contain only admissible evidence and, like pleadings, must be as short as possible and include only relevant material. If the affidavit is unduly lengthy, it may be struck out. Affidavits must not, for example, contain reference to "without prejudice" negotiations, which are inadmissible.

2. Exhibits

If the deponent wishes to refer to a document, this is made the subject of an exhibit. In the affidavit, the deponent states "There is now produced and shown to me marked 'J.S. 1'." The exhibit is attached to a certificate bearing the title of the action and the words "This is the exhibit marked 'J.S. 1' referred to in the affidavit of John Smith sworn before me, the 1st May 1991" followed by the signature of the solicitor/ Commissioner for Oaths.

Practice Direction (Evidence: Documents) [1983] 1 WLR 922 sets out in detail the practice as to exhibits, the relevant parts of which are as follows:

(a) Markings generally

Where space allows, the directions as to marking (see above) apply to the first page of every exhibit.

(b) Documents other than letters

(i) Clearly legible photographic copies of original documents may be exhibited instead of the originals provided the originals are made available for inspection by the other parties before the hearing and by the judge at the hearing.

(ii) Any document which the court is being asked to construe or enforce, or the trusts of which it is being asked to vary, should be separately exhibited, and should not be included in a bundle with other documents. Any such document should bear the exhibit mark directly, and not on a flysheet attached to it.

(iii) Court documents, such as probates, letters of administration, orders, affidavits or pleadings, should never be exhibited. Office copies of such documents prove themselves.

(iv) Where a number of documents are contained in one exhibit, a front page must be attached, setting out a list of the documents, with dates, which the exhibit contains, and the bundle must be securely fastened. The traditional method of securing is by tape, with the knot sealed (under the modern practice) by means of wafers; but any means of securing the bundle (except by staples) is acceptable, provided that it does not interfere with the perusal of the documents and it cannot readily be undone.

(v) This direction does not affect the current practice in relation to scripts in probate matters, or to an affidavit of due execution of a will.

(c) Letters

(i) Copies of individual letters should not be made separate exhibits, but they should be collected together and exhibited in a bundle or bundles. The letters must be arranged in correct sequence with the earliest at the top, and properly paged in accordance with paragraph (d) below. They must be firmly secured together in the manner indicated in paragraph (b) above.

(ii) When original letters, or original letters and copies of replies, are exhibited as one bundle, the exhibit must have a front page attached, stating that the bundle consists of so many original letters and so many copies. As before, the letters and copies must be arranged in correct sequence and properly paged.

(d) Paging of documentary exhibits

Any exhibit containing several pages must be paged consecutively at centre bottom.

(e) Copies of documents generally

It is the responsibility of the solicitor by whom any affidavit is filed to ensure that every page of every exhibit is fully and easily legible. In many cases photocopies of documents, particularly of telex messages, are not. In all cases of difficulty, typed copies of the illegible document (paged with "a" numbers) should be included.

113

(f) Exhibits bound up with affidavit

Exhibits must not be bound up with, or otherwise attached to, the affidavit itself.

(g) Exhibits other than documents

The principles are as follows:

(i) The exhibit must be clearly marked with the exhibit mark in such a manner that there is no likelihood of the contents being separated; and

(ii) where the exhibit itself consists of more than one item (eg a cassette in a plastic box), each and every separate part of the exhibit must similarly be separately marked with at least enough of the usual exhibit mark to ensure precise identification.

This is particularly important in cases where there are a number of similar exhibits which fall to be compared. Accordingly:

(i) The formal exhibit marking should, so far as practicable, be written on the article itself in an appropriate manner (many fabrics can be directly marked with an indelible pen), or, if this is not possible, on a separate slip which is securely attached to the article in such a manner that it is not easily removable. (NB Items attached by Sellotape or similar means are readily removable.) If the article is then enclosed in a container, the number of the exhibit should appear on the outside of the container unless it is transparent and the number is readily visible.

Alternatively, the formal exhibit marking may be written on the container, or, if this is not possible, on a separate slip securely attached to the container. If this is done, then either:

- the number of the exhibit and, if there is room, the short name and number of the case, the name of the deponent and the date of the affidavit must be written on the exhibit itself and on each separate part thereof; or

- all these particulars must appear on a slip securely attached to the article itself and to each separate part thereof.

(ii) If the article, or part of the article, is too small to be marked in accordance with the foregoing provisions, it must be enclosed in a sealed transparent container of such a nature that it could not be reconstituted once opened, and the relevant slip containing the exhibit mark must be inserted in such container so as to be plainly visible. An enlarged photograph or photographs showing the relevant characteristics of each such exhibit will usually be required to be separately exhibited.

(h) Numbering

Where a deponent deposes to more than one affidavit to which there are exhibits in any one matter, the numbering of such exhibits should run consecutively throughout, and not begin again with each affidavit.

(i) Reference to documents already forming part of an exhibit

Where a deponent wishes to refer to a document already exhibited to some other deponent's affidavit, he should not also exhibit it to his own affidavit.

(j) Multiplicity of documents

Where, by the time of the hearing, exhibits or affidavits have become numerous, they should be put in a consolidated bundle, or file or files, and be paged consecutively throughout in the top right hand corner, affidavits and exhibits being in separate bundles or files.

3. Jurat

An affidavit must be signed by the deponent who must swear on oath before a solicitor or Commissioner for Oaths that its contents are correct. Note that the party's own solicitor must not administer the oath, nor a solicitor from the same firm. The statement that the affidavit has been sworn etc. is called the jurat. The jurat must contain the address where the affidavit is sworn. Furthermore, it must follow on immediately after the text of the affidavit. Consequently, the text must not finish on one page, with the jurat on the top of the next page.

The form is as follows:

```
SWORN at 1 Regents Street, London W1      )
the 1st day of May 1991 before me,        )   Alan Jones
John Henry Blenkinsop (signature)         )   (signature)
Solicitor
```

More than one deponent can make one affidavit, in which case the form of jurat depends on whether all the deponents swear the affidavit together. If they do, the jurat will be:

```
SWORN by both the above-named deponents at )
1 Regents Street, London W1 before me,     )   (both
John Henry Blenkinsop (signature)          )   signatures)
Solicitor
```

If they swear the affidavit separately, the jurats will look like this:

```
SWORN by the above-named deponent         )
Alan Jones at 1 Regents Street,           )   Alan Jones
London W 1 the 1st day of May 1991        )   (signature)
before me,                                )
John Henry Blenkinsop (signature)
Solicitor
SWORN by the above-named deponent         )
John Smith at 3 Regents Street,           )   John Smith
London W1 the 2nd day of May 1991         )   (signature)
before me,                                )
Peter Harris (signature)
Commissioner for Oaths.
```

Where the deponent is illiterate or blind, the person administering the oath must certify in the jurat that:

(a) the affidavit was read in his presence to the deponent,
(b) the deponent seemed perfectly to understand it, and
(c) the deponent made his signature or mark in his presence.

In the case of an affirmation, the jurat is identical, save for the replacement of the word "Sworn" by the word "Affirmed".

After the jurat, the affidavit must be indorsed with a note showing on whose behalf it is filed and the dates of swearing and filing. Even though this involves some duplication, it is a prerequisite of filing or using the affidavit: O 41 r 9(5).

4. Form

Order 66 applies to affidavits, as to which see Chapter 1, page 8. In addition, affidavits must be bound in book form (though not with thick plastic strips, or anything which would hamper filing). Whether or not both sides of the paper are used, the printed, written or typed sides of paper must be numbered consecutively.

(a) Alterations etc.

If the body or jurat of an affidavit contains any interlineation, erasure or other alteration, it may not be used without the court's leave, unless the person before whom it is sworn has initialled the alteration and, in the case of an erasure, has re-written in the margin of the affidavit any words or figures written on the erasure and has signed or initialled them. Where the affidavit is sworn at the Central Office or any other office of the Supreme Court, the official stamp of that office may be substituted for the signature or initials.

The layout of an affidavit is, therefore, as follows:

Pltf: W Shakespeare: 1st: 1.5.91

IN THE HIGH COURT OF JUSTICE

QUEEN'S BENCH DIVISION

BETWEEN: SOLILOQUY THEATRES (a firm)   <u>Plaintiff</u>

and

EDWARD SLAPPER and others   <u>Defendants</u>

I, William Shakespeare, of Hathaway Cottage, 9 Hamlet Street, Stratford-upon-Avon, Warwickshire, actor, make oath and say as follows:

1.   I am an actor employed by the Plaintiff firm, and have been so employed for the past 4 years. I am duly authorised to make this affidavit on the Plaintiff's behalf. My duties include the hiring of staff, including make-up artists.

117

2. On the 15th April 1990, I interviewed the First Defendant for the job of part-time make-up artist and thought him a suitable applicant. I am informed by John Derby, one of the partners of the Plaintiff firm, and believe, that the First Defendant was engaged to work by the Plaintiff firm with effect from 21st April 1990.

3. There is now produced and shown to me marked "W.S.1" a copy of a contract of employment between the Plaintiff and the First Defendant. I witnessed the First Defendant's signature on the contract, and I confirm that my signature appears at the bottom of the contract next to the First Defendant's.

SWORN at 1 High Street, Coventry)
the 1st day of May 1991, before me,) William Shakespeare
Charles Dickens (signature)) (signature)
A Commissioner for Oaths

5. County court

By CCR O 20 r 10(1), subject to a number of matters, the following High Court provisions apply:

(a) the form and contents of an affidavit;
(b) the making of an affidavit by two or more deponents or by a blind or illiterate deponent;
(c) the use of any affidavit which contains an interlineation, erasure or other alteration or is otherwise defective;
(d) the striking out of any matter which is scandalous, irrelevant or otherwise oppressive;
(e) the insufficiency of an affidavit sworn before any agent, partner or clerk of a party's solicitor; and
(f) the making and marking of exhibits to an affidavit.

The other formal requirement in the county court (CCR O 20 r 10(3)) is that every affidavit must be marked in the top right hand corner of the first page and in the top right hand corner of the back sheet with:

(a) the party on whose behalf the affidavit is filed;
(b) the initials and surname of the deponent;
(c) the number of the affidavit in relation to the deponent;
(d) the date on which it is sworn;
(e) the date on which it is filed.

Example

Plaintiff: R.M. Wilson
2nd Sworn 13.7.91
Filed 18.7.91

Hearsay

Unlike the High Court, in all cases in the county court an affidavit may be used notwithstanding that it contains statements of information or belief. This rule applies unless the court specifically orders otherwise. The weight to be attached to a statement in an affidavit is a matter for the court. Accordingly, any matter of importance should be deposed to by someone with direct knowledge.

However, the affidavit must make clear which facts are within the deponent's knowledge and which are based on information or belief. The means of knowledge and the sources and grounds of the information or belief, as the case may be, must be given.

Appendix A

Parties

This Appendix sets out how various parties should be described in the heading of the pleading. Capital letters should be used.

1. Individual

An individual should be described by his or her full names, so far as these are known, and without the title Mr., Mrs. etc.

Thus: "ALAN PETER JONES"

If the full names are not known, such names or initials as are known will suffice, but in this case, the sex of the person should be made clear, by use of brackets after the name, or by using Mr., Mrs. etc.

Thus: "A. P. JONES (male)" or "MR. A. P. JONES"

A woman's marital status is no longer given.

In actions in the Queen's Bench Division, if a female party changes her name on marriage after the commencement of the proceedings by or against her, a written notice of the change of name must be filed by her or on her behalf at the Action Department, Central Office, or at the district registry, and a copy must be served on all other parties. In the title of the proceedings the new name must, after the notice has been filed, be substituted and the former name be mentioned in brackets (*Queen's Bench Masters' Practice Direction 17* para 4).

Thus: "ANNE SMITH (formerly ANNE BUTCHER)"

A peer or knight should be given his title. For example:

- The Most Noble Charles Henry Duke of Yorkshire
- The Most Honourable Michael Brian Marquess of Brighton
- The Right Honourable Peter Earl of Taunton
- The Right Honourable Walter Baron Enright

121

- The Right Honourable Derek Pears, commonly called Lord Victoria
- Sir Eric Piles

2. Sole trader

An individual who is the sole proprietor of a business with a trading name, and who is suing or sued in connection with that business should be described as follows:

"ALAN PETER JONES (trading as SPOTLESS ANTIQUES)"

3. Company

The full correct name of the company should be given, as follows:

"JONES BROTHERS LIMITED"

"SMITH INDUSTRIES PLC"

Note, the abbreviation LTD should *not* be used for a private company, but PLC for a public company should.

In Wales, the equivalent of Limited (Ltd) is Cyfyngedig, abbreviation Cyf., and the equivalent of PLC is CCC.

If the true legal description of a corporate or other body is not apparent from its name, the description should be stated. Thus: "JENKINS HOLDING COMPANY (A company limited by guarantee)".

Remember that, in the pleading, a company being a legal person, should preferably be referred to in the singular, as the Plaintiff or Defendant, and as "it" – rather than as the Plaintiffs or Defendants, and as "they". Some people refer to a company in the plural, but this could lead to confusion in certain cases between the company and the individuals behind it.

If a limited company changes its name after commencement of proceedings by or against it, written notice of the change of name must be filed at the Action Department, Central Office, or at the district registry, and a copy must be served on all other parties. In the title of the proceedings, the new name is thereafter substituted and the former name mentioned in brackets (*Queen's Bench Masters' Practice Direction 17* para 3).

Thus: "MILLSTONE LIMITED (formerly called WITCHES LIMITED)"

If the company has changed its name before proceedings have been commenced, the fact should be mentioned in the body of the pleading.

Example

POTATO VIDEO LIMITED	<u>Plaintiff</u>
and	
JOHN SMITH	<u>Defendant</u>

STATEMENT OF CLAIM

1. By an agreement made between the Plaintiff, then called Snoring Television Limited, and the Defendant, . . . The Plaintiff changed its name by special resolution on the 1st April 1991.

4. Partnerships

The name of the partnership should be given, followed by the words "a firm", as follows:

"GREEN BROTHERS (a firm)"

Sometimes the words "suing as a firm" or "sued as a firm" are used.

5. Persons under disability

(a) Minors

Where the plaintiff is a minor, he sues by his next friend, and is referred to as follows:

MATTHEW JOHNSON (a minor, by HARRY JOHNSON, his father and next friend)	<u>Plaintiff</u>

If the next friend is not a parent, his description is not given in the title.

In the Chancery Division, the next friend's name is not set out in the title but in the body of the Writ or Originating Summons:

MATTHEW JOHNSON (a minor)	<u>Plaintiff</u>
and	
PETER SMITH	<u>Defendant</u>

STATEMENT OF CLAIM

1. The Plaintiff is a minor who brings these proceedings by Harry Johnson, his father and next friend.

The Supreme Court Practice suggests that in the Queen's Bench Division it is the practice to allege in the Statement of Claim that the Plaintiff is an infant suing by his next friend, as well as in the title. There appears to be no rule or practice direction requiring this, but it seems to be sensible practice.

Where the defendant is a minor, he defends by his guardian *ad litem*, and is referred to as follows (in all courts);

DERRICK PEARS   <u>Plaintiff</u>
and
MICHAEL SQUEAKER (a minor by SEAN ENRIGHT
his guardian ad litem) <u>Defendant</u>

(b) Mental patients

Where the plaintiff is a patient under the Mental Health Act 1983, the Writ or Originating Summons should not describe him as a patient, but his next friend should be referred to, as follows:

JOHN HARRIS (by MARY JONES his next friend)
<u>Plaintiff</u>

The Statement of Claim should allege that the plaintiff is a patient.

Where the Defendant is a patient, after acknowledgement of service, the title reads:

JOY GREEN (by BARRY BROWN her guardian ad litem)
<u>Defendant</u>

In the case of a Third Party Notice or Defence and Counterclaim, it is necessary to divide up the title as follows:

IN THE HIGH COURT OF JUSTICE   1991 V No. 8794
QUEEN'S BENCH DIVISION

BETWEEN: VERMILION LIMITED <u>Plaintiff</u>
      and
JOY GREEN (by BARRY BROWN her guardian ad litem)
            <u>Defendant</u>

AND BETWEEN:

    JOY GREEN (by BARRY BROWN her next friend)
            <u>Plaintiff</u>
  and
    PATRICK McDONALD <u>Third Party</u>

6. Corporate bodies

The following are either corporate bodies who may sue or be sued in their corporate name, or are effectively treated as such.

(a) Health authorities

Under the National Health Service Act 1977 (Sch 5 para 8), each of the following bodies:

- Regional Health Authority
- District Health Authority
- Special Health Authority
- Family Practitioner Committee

(b) Trade unions

By s 2(1)(c) Trade Union and Labour Relations Act 1974, a trade union is capable of suing and being sued in its own name in all cases.

(c) Utility companies

Gas: British Gas PLC.

Water: the National Rivers Authority or the statutory water undertakers (companies) formed after the coming into force of the Water Act 1989.

Electricity: the companies formed following the coming into force of the Electricity Act 1989 are:

Taking over from the former Area Boards

- London Electricity plc
- SEEBOARD plc
- Southern Electric plc
- South Western Electricity plc
- Eastern Electricity plc
- East Midlands Electricity plc
- Midlands Electricity plc
- South Wales Electricity plc
- Manweb plc
- Yorkshire Electricity Group plc
- Northern Electric plc
- NORWEB plc

Taking over from Generating Board

- National Power plc
- PowerGen plc
- The National Grid Company plc
- Nuclear Electric plc

Taking over from Electricity Council

- Electricity Association Services Limited
- National Power plc
- Electra Brands Limited

The Atomic Energy Authority is a body corporate.

Post Office and Telephones: By s 6 and Sch 1 Post Office Act 1969, the Post Office is a public authority, unconnected with the Crown, and is a body corporate, called "The Post Office".

Telecommunications: British Telecommunications plc.

(d) Transport

The following are statutorily constituted bodies corporate:

- London Regional Transport (London Regional Transport Act 1984)
- British Railways Board (Transport Act 1962)
- British Transport Docks Board (Transport Act 1962)
- British Waterways Board (Transport Act 1962)

(e) Local authorities

County Council: The County Council of Borsetshire

District Council: The District Council of South-East Borsetshire

City Council: The City Council of Barchester

Parish Council: The Parish Council of Westleigh

Community Council: The Community Council of Barton

City of London: The Mayor and Commonalty and Citizens of the City of London

London Borough: The Mayor and Councillors of the:

- Royal Borough of Kensington and Chelsea
- City of Westminster
- Borough of Lewisham

(f) Building societies

An incorporated building society sues in its registered name, eg The BORSETSHIRE BUILDING SOCIETY.

An unincorporated building society sues by its trustees or officers as representing its members.

(g) Friendly societies

Where the trustees or authorised officers of a registered friendly society bring or defend proceedings (under s 103(1) Friendly

Societies Act 1974), they sue or are sued in their proper names without any other description than the title of their office.

Thus: "John Jones and Peter Thomson (Trustees of the South Melchester Friendly Society)".

In proceedings brought under the Friendly Societies Act 1974 by a member or person claiming through a member, a registered society or branch may be sued in the name (as defendant) of any officer or person who receives contributions or issues policies on behalf of the society, eg "John Jones (on behalf of the Eastern Branch of the South Melchester Friendly Society)" (s 103(2) Friendly Societies Act 1974).

In other cases, or where the individuals names are unknown, the society may be sued as "The South Melchester Friendly Society (registered under the Friendly Societies Act 1974)."

If the friendly society is unregistered, it sues or is sued in a representative capacity, thus:

"John Jones and Peter Thomson (on behalf of themselves and all other members of the South Melchester Friendly Society)."

7. Charities

Where the validity of a charitable bequest to a charity is in issue, the trustees of the charity are proper parties. Otherwise the Attorney-General represents the charity. He is described as "Her Majesty's Attorney-General".

The Charity Commissioners are described as "The Charity Commissioners for England and Wales".

The Official Custodian for Charities is a party under that title.

8. Church

The Church Commissioners are a body corporate, suing and sued as "The Church Commissioners for England".

A Parochial Church Council is a body corporate called, for example, "The Parochial Church Council of the Parish of St. John's, Botley".

9. Trustees

The trustees may simply be named in the title and the fact they are trustees referred to in the body of the pleading. Alternatively, the title may refer to their status. For example:

"John Peters (Trustee of the Will of Joan Smith, deceased)".

127

10. Executors and administrators

These are described as follows:

"John Smith and Peter Morris (Executors of the Will of Joan Smith, deceased)".

"John Smith (Administrator of the Estate of Joan Smith, deceased)".

11. Clubs and societies

If they are incorporated, they may sue and be sued in their corporate name.

The proprietor of an unincorporated proprietary club may sue and be sued in his own name or the name of the club. Two or more proprietors may be treated as a partnership.

In the case of an unincorporated members' club, if property is vested in trustees, the trustees are the proper parties. One or more members may sue or be sued as representing the others. For example:

"Andrew Miller and Mark Porter (on their own behalf and on behalf of all other members of the Borsetshire Motorcycle Club)".

12. The Crown

Proceedings involving the Crown are either brought by or against the appropriate government department (eg, Ministry of Defence) or, where there is none, or there is doubt, the Attorney-General ("Her Majesty's Attorney-General").

The current list of Authorised Government Departments and their solicitors and addresses for service is as follows:

Authorised Government Department	Solicitors and Addresses for Service
• Advisory, Conciliation and Arbitration Service	The Treasury Solicitor Queen Anne's Chambers
• Board of Trade	28 Broadway
• Building Societies Commission	Westminster London SW1H 9JS
• Crown Prosecution Service	
• Ministry of Defence	
• Department of Education and Science	
• Department of Employment	
• Department of Energy	

Authorised Government Department	*Solicitors and Addresses for Service*
• Department of Environment[a]	
• Export Credits Guarantee Department	
• Director General of Fair Trading	
• Director General of Gas Supply	
• Registry of Friendly Societies	
• Health and Safety Commission	
• Health and Safety Executive	
• Department of Health	
• Home Office	
• Office of the Minister for the Civil Service	
• Department of National Savings	
• Northern Ireland Office	
• Office of Arts and Libraries	
• Office of Population Censuses and Surveys	
• Public Works Loan Board	
• Serious Fraud Office	
• Department of Social Security[b]	
• Her Majesty's Stationery Office	
• Director General of Telecommunications	
• Department of Trade and Industry	
• Training Commission[c]	
• Department of Transport	
• Her Majesty's Treasury	
• Welsh Office[d]	
• Ministry of Agriculture, Fisheries and Food[d]	Solicitor to the Ministry of Agriculture, Fisheries and Food 55 Whitehall London SW1A 2EY
• Forestry Commission	

Authorised Government Department	*Solicitors and Addresses for Service*
● Intervention Board for Agricultural Produce	
● Commissioners of Customs and Excise	Solicitor for the Customs and Excise New King's Beam House 22 Upper Ground London SE1 9PJ
● Commissioners of Inland Revenue	Solicitor of Inland Revenue Somerset House London WC2R 1LB
● Crown Estate Commissioners	Solicitor to the Crown Estate Commissioners Crown Estate Office 16 Carlton House Terrace London SW1Y 5AH

Notes

(a) Any proceedings relating to matters transferred from the Land Commission by s 1(3) Land Commission (Dissolution) Act 1971 are dealt with by the Solicitor to the Department of the Environment, 2 Marsham Street, London SW1P 3EB.

(b) The following matters are dealt with by the Solicitor to the Department of Health and Social Security, Ray House, 6 St Andrew Street, London EC4A 3AD (rather than the Treasury Solicitor, who deals with all other matters for the department of Social Security):

   (i) adjudications under legislation governing war pensions and social security by the Secretary of State for Social Security, a tribunal or other adjudicating authority, and matters relating to the administration of benefit under such legislation;

   (ii) recovery of monies under and matters arising from non-receipt of benefit under the legislation mentioned in (i) above and cases stated under s 111 Magistrates' Courts Act 1980 in connection with prosecutions under such legislation;

   (iii) matters arising under the Social Fund (Pt III Social Security Act 1986); and

   (iv) determinations by the Occupational Pensions Board.

(c) The Training Commission was dissolved on 16 November 1989 by s 22 Employment Act 1989.

(d) Matters in Wales for which the Ministry of Agriculture, Fisheries and Food is responsible in England are handled by the Solicitor for the Ministry of Agriculture at 55 Whitehall.

13. Police

Actions in tort are brought against the Chief Officer of Police for the relevant police area.

In respect of other claims, actions by and against the Metropolitan Police are brought in the name of "The Receiver for the Metropolitan Police District".

In other areas, proceedings are in the name of the police committee, and are brought by or against the clerk of the council or the town clerk, as representing the committee.

Appendix B

Examples of pleadings

The remainder of the book comprises examples of pleadings. In each case, a full set of pleadings is set out. Although they are not intended as precedents, they do show the reader how complete sets of pleadings look. The types of claim are fairly straightforward, and are likely to be found in general (rather than specialist) practice.

In mentioning precedents, it is worth sounding a note of caution about their use. There are a number of major works on precedents of pleadings. It is very unusual to find a precedent in which the facts pleaded are precisely the same as one's own case. Generally, it is preferable to attempt to draft a pleading without a precedent, and perhaps use a precedent book later to check the wording of a particular allegation. That way one learns the technique of pleading by experience. Remember also that precedent books are not infallible.

Contents

1. Negligence – personal injuries – road accident

(i) Statement of Claim

IN THE HIGH COURT OF JUSTICE	1991 C No. 5467

QUEEN'S BENCH DIVISION

(Writ issued the 23rd day of May 1991)

BETWEEN:

JEREMY CRUNCH   <u>Plaintiff</u>

and

MONSTER TRUCKS LIMITED   <u>Defendant</u>

STATEMENT OF CLAIM

1. At all material times the Defendant employed one Peter Barker as a van driver.

2. At about 1.30 p.m. on the 4th December 1989, the Plaintiff was driving his Rover motor car, registration no. G567 ABC in a northerly direction along the highway known as Rosetree Avenue, Richmond in the County of Surrey, when a Ford Transit van registration no. B435 NMH owned by the Defendant and being driven by the said Barker, in the course of his said employment, emerged from Jamaica Grove intending to turn right into Rosetree Avenue and collided with the Plaintiff's said motor car.

3. The said collision was caused by the negligence of the said Barker.

PARTICULARS OF NEGLIGENCE

(i) Emerging from a minor road into a major road without giving priority to traffic on the major road;

(ii) Failing to observe or heed the Give Way sign at the end of Jamaica Grove;

(iii) Driving too fast in the circumstances;

(iv) Failing to keep any or any proper lookout;

(v) Failing to steer, brake or otherwise control the said van so as to avoid colliding with the said motor car.

4. By reason of the aforesaid, the Plaintiff has suffered pain and injury, loss and damage.

PARTICULARS OF INJURY

(a) Whiplash injury to the neck;

(b) Fracture of two vertebrae;

    (c)   Severe bruising to the right arm and leg;

    (d)   Lacerations of the right cheek and forehead;

    (e)   Shock.

The Plaintiff was born on the 22nd August 1955.

PARTICULARS OF SPECIAL DAMAGE

Repairs to damaged car − £1,600.75

Replacement of torn pullover and trousers − £95

Net loss of earnings from 4th December 1989 until 5th March 1990 − £4,150.

5.   Further, the Plaintiff is entitled to and claims interest on such damages as he is awarded pursuant to Section 35A of the Supreme Court Act 1981 at such rate and for such period as this Honourable Court shall think fit.

AND the Plaintiff claims:

1.   Damages;

2.   Interest thereon pursuant to paragraph 5 hereof to be assessed.

Served the 6th day of September 1991, by Gunge & Co. of 15 High Street, Richmond, Surrey, Solicitors for the Plaintiff.

Note

A medical report and schedule of special damages will be served with the Statement of Claim.

(ii) Defence and Counterclaim

IN THE HIGH COURT OF JUSTICE　　　　　　**1991 C No. 5467**

QUEEN'S BENCH DIVISION

BETWEEN:　　　　　　　　JEREMY CRUNCH　　　　　<u>Plaintiff</u>
　　　　　　　　　　　　　　and
　　　　　　　　　MONSTER TRUCKS LIMITED　　　<u>Defendant</u>

DEFENCE AND COUNTERCLAIM

DEFENCE

1.   Paragraph 1 of the Statement of Claim is admitted.

2. Save that it is admitted that at the time and place alleged a collision took place between the vehicles pleaded, and denied that the said Barker was acting in the course of his employment with the Defendant, no admissions are made as to Paragraph 2 of the Statement of Claim.

3. It is denied that the said collision was caused by the negligence of the said Barker as alleged in Paragraph 3 of the Statement of Claim or at all.

4. Further or alternatively, the said collision was caused wholly or in part by the negligence of the Plaintiff.

PARTICULARS OF NEGLIGENCE

(i) Driving too fast in all the circumstances;

(ii) Failing to heed the presence of the said van, which had emerged slowly and carefully from Jamaica Avenue, having made sure that it was safe to do so;

(iii) Driving his said car whilst using a hand-held car telephone;

(iv) Failing to steer, brake or otherwise control his said car so as to avoid colliding with the Defendant's van.

5. No admissions are made as to the pain, injury, loss and damage alleged in Paragraph 4 of the Statement of Claim or at all.

6. It is denied that the Plaintiff is entitled to the relief claimed or any relief.

7. Alternatively, the Defendant will seek to set off against the Plaintiff's claim such sums as it recovers under its Counterclaim herein, in extinction or diminution thereof.

COUNTERCLAIM

8. The Defendant repeats Paragraph 4 of the Defence.

9. By reason of the said collision, the Defendant has suffered loss and damage.

PARTICULARS OF SPECIAL DAMAGE

Cost of repairs to Defendant's van – £1,250.

10. Further, the Defendant is entitled to and claims interest on such damages as it is awarded pursuant to Section 35A of the Supreme Court Act 1981 at such rate and for such period as this Honourable Court thinks fit.

AND the Defendant counterclaims:

1. Damages;

2. Interest thereon to be assessed.

Served the 30th day of September 1991 etc.

Notes

- The Defence denies that the driver was acting in the course of his employment. This is important since the driver has not been joined as a Defendant. This is the sort of point which "calls out" for a Request for Further and Better Particulars.
- If the driver had been injured in the accident and wished to counterclaim damages, he would have to be joined in the proceedings as a Plaintiff to the Counterclaim.

(iii) Request for Further and Better Particulars of Defence and Counterclaim

IN THE HIGH COURT OF JUSTICE   **1991 C No. 5467**

QUEEN'S BENCH DIVISION

BETWEEN: JEREMY CRUNCH   <u>Plaintiff</u>
                                    and
                    MONSTER TRUCKS LIMITED   <u>Defendant</u>

**REQUEST FOR FURTHER AND BETTER PARTICULARS OF
DEFENCE AND COUNTERCLAIM**

<u>Under Paragraph 2</u>

Of "it is . . . denied that the said Barker was acting in the course of his employment with the Defendant . . ."

State

1. Where the said Barker was driving from and to at the time of the said collision;
2. What was the purpose of his journey;
3. All facts and matters relied upon in support of the contention that he was not acting in the course of his employment with the Defendant.

Served the 20th day of October 1991 etc

(iv) *Further and Better Particulars of Defence and Counterclaim*

IN THE HIGH COURT OF JUSTICE   1991 C No. 5467

QUEEN'S BENCH DIVISION

BETWEEN: JEREMY CRUNCH   Plaintiff
                                    and
                    MONSTER TRUCKS LIMITED   Defendant

FURTHER AND BETTER PARTICULARS OF DEFENCE AND COUNTERCLAIM PURSUANT TO REQUEST SERVED THE 20th OCTOBER 1991

Under Paragraph 2

Of "it is . . . denied that the said Barker was acting in the course of his employment with the Defendant . . ."

Request

State

1. Where the said Barker was driving from and to at the time of the said collision;

2. What was the purpose of his journey;

3. All facts and matters relied upon in support of the contention that he was not acting in the course of his employment with the Defendant.

Reply

1. From East Sheen to Twickenham;

2. To visit his dentist;

3. The said Barker was employed to deliver parcels. He was given permission to visit his dentist for a dental appointment during his lunch break, and to use the Respondent's van.

Served the 14th day of November 1991 etc.

(v) Reply and Defence to Counterclaim

IN THE HIGH COURT OF JUSTICE   **1991 C No. 5467**

QUEEN'S BENCH DIVISION

BETWEEN: JEREMY CRUNCH   <u>Plaintiff</u>

and

MONSTER TRUCKS LIMITED   <u>Defendant</u>

REPLY AND DEFENCE TO COUNTERCLAIM

REPLY

1. Save insofar as it contains admissions, the Plaintiff joins issue with the Defence.

2. It is denied that the Plaintiff acted negligently, as alleged in Paragraph 4 of the Defence or at all.

DEFENCE TO COUNTERCLAIM

3. Paragraph 8 of the Counterclaim is denied.

4. No admission is made as to Paragraph 9 of the Counterclaim.

5. It is denied that the Defendant is entitled to the relief counterclaimed or any relief.

Served the 20th day of October 1991 etc.

2. Professional negligence – claim against solicitor – failure to issue Writ within limitation period

(i) Statement of Claim

IN THE HIGH COURT OF JUSTICE	**1991 B No. 7345**
QUEEN'S BENCH DIVISION	

BETWEEN:

WALTER BAILEY <u>Plaintiff</u>

and

HAROLD SCOUSE <u>Defendant</u>

STATEMENT OF CLAIM

1. The Defendant is and was at all material times a Solicitor practising under the style Scouse & Co. at 345 Green Lane, Liverpool.

2. On the 24th June 1990, the Plaintiff consulted the Defendant at his said office for professional advice about recovery of a sum of £6,000 owed to him by one Robert Jones.

3. Thereafter, the Plaintiff instructed the Defendant to act for him, for reward, to recover the said sum by commencing proceedings.

4. It was an implied term of the said agreement that the Defendant would act for the Plaintiff using reasonable skill and care, inter alia in commencing the said proceedings.

5. In breach of the said term and/or negligently, the Defendant failed to take any action to protect the Plaintiff's position prior to the Plaintiff's claim becoming statute-barred by virtue of Section 5 of the Limitation Act 1980.

PARTICULARS

The Defendant failed to issue a Writ within 6 years from the date when the Plaintiff's cause of action against the said Jones arose, that date being the 2nd January 1985, the date under the loan when the money was to be repaid.

6. By reason of the Defendant's said breach of contract and/or negligence, the Plaintiff has lost the right to recover the said sum from the said Jones, and has thereby suffered loss and damage.

PARTICULARS OF SPECIAL DAMAGE

Amount paid to the Defendant on account of costs – £750.

143

The Plaintiff had a good prospect of recovering the said sum of £6,000 plus statutory interest from the 2nd January 1985.

7. Further, the Plaintiff is entitled to and claims interest on such damages as he is awarded pursuant to Section 35A of the Supreme Court Act 1981 at such rate and for such period as this Honourable Court thinks fit.

AND the Plaintiff claims:

1. Damages;

2. Interest pursuant to Paragraph 7 hereof to be assessed.

Served etc.

(ii) Defence

IN THE HIGH COURT OF JUSTICE   **1991 B No. 7345**

QUEEN'S BENCH DIVISION

BETWEEN: WALTER BAILEY   Plaintiff
                                       and
                            HAROLD SCOUSE   Defendant

DEFENCE

1. Paragraphs 1 to 4 of the Statement of Claim are admitted.

2. The Defendant advised the Plaintiff:

    (i)   That the said sum of £6,000 would, in the light of the correspondence passing between the Plaintiff and the said Jones, be held to be a gift to the said Jones;

    (ii) That it would be a waste of money for the Plaintiff to commence proceedings;

    (iii) That the Plaintiff should go away and think about the Defendant's advice, and that, if he still wanted to issue proceedings, he should return to the Defendant to give him further instructions.

3. Pursuant to the said advice, the Plaintiff went away and did not return or give the Defendant further instructions.

4. In the premises, whilst it is admitted that the Defendant did not issue a Writ, it is denied that he acted in breach of the said term or negligently as alleged in Paragraph 5 of the Statement of Claim or at all.

5. It is denied that the Plaintiff has suffered loss and damage as alleged or at all. Without prejudice to the foregoing, (i) the Defendant's costs were a reasonable sum for the work carried out; (ii) the Plaintiff would not have recovered the alleged or any sum from the said Jones.

6. In the premises, it is denied that the Plaintiff is entitled to the relief claimed or any relief.

Served etc.

3. Occupiers' liability – personal injuries

(i) Statement of Claim

IN THE HIGH COURT OF JUSTICE   1991 E No. 5674

QUEEN'S BENCH DIVISION

BETWEEN: THE RIGHT HONOURABLE WALTER BARON ENRIGHT

Plaintiff

and

NELLIS AND SALMON (A Firm)   Defendant

STATEMENT OF CLAIM

1. At all material times the Defendant was the proprietor and occupier of a restaurant known as Salmonellas, 45 Kings Street, London SW17.

2. On the 16th September 1990, the Plaintiff was a customer in the said restaurant. At about 8.30 p.m. he was looking for the lavatory at the rear of the restaurant, and had started to descend a flight of stairs believing the lavatory to be at the bottom, when the top stair collapsed, and the Plaintiff fell down the staircase.

3. The Plaintiff was at all material times a visitor of the Defendant within the meaning of the Occupiers' Liability Act 1957.

4. The Plaintiff's said fall was caused by the negligence and or breach of the common duty of care under Section 2 of the said Act by the Defendant, its servants or agents.

PARTICULARS

(i)   Causing or permitting the said top stair to be in a defective condition;

(ii)   Failing to inspect the said staircase and/or keep it in repair;

(iii)   Failing to warn the Plaintiff of the defective nature of the said staircase.

5. By reason of the aforesaid, the Plaintiff has suffered injury, loss and damage.

PARTICULARS OF INJURY

(a)   Comminuted fracture of the right fibula

(b)   Bruising of the right lower leg and ankle.

The Plaintiff was born on the 4th May 1943.

PARTICULARS OF SPECIAL DAMAGE

Replacement of damaged suit − £550.

Medical expenses − £2,600.

6. Further, the Plaintiff is entitled to and claims interest on such damages as he is awarded pursuant to Section 35A of the Supreme Court Act 1981 at such rate and for such period as this Honourable Court thinks fit.

AND the Plaintiff claims;

1. Damages;
2. Interest under Paragraph 6 hereof to be assessed.

Served the 5th day of December 1991 etc.

(ii) Defence

IN THE HIGH COURT OF JUSTICE   **1991 E No. 5674**

QUEEN'S BENCH DIVISION

BETWEEN: THE RIGHT HONOURABLE WALTER BARON ENRIGHT

<u>Plaintiff</u>

and

NELLIS AND SALMON (A Firm)   <u>Defendant</u>

DEFENCE

1. Save that no admissions are made as to how or why the Plaintiff fell down the said staircase, Paragraphs 1 to 3 of the Statement of Claim are admitted.
2. It is denied that the Defendant was negligent or in breach of the common duty of care under Section 2 of the Occupier's Liability Act 1957 as alleged in Paragraph 4 of the Statement of Claim or at all. At the top of the said staircase, the Defendant had placed a notice saying in large letters: "Warning − unsafe staircase, do not use − toilets first left down the corridor."
3. Further or alternatively, the Plaintiff's fall was caused wholly or in part by his own negligence.

PARTICULARS OF NEGLIGENCE

(i) Failing to read or take heed of the said notice.
(ii) Descending the said staircase, having been warned that it was unsafe to do so.

147

4. Further in the premises, the Plaintiff impliedly consented to running the risk of injury by descending the staircase.

5. No admissions are made as to the alleged or any injury, loss or damage.

6. It is denied that the Plaintiff is entitled to the relief claimed or any relief.

Served the 22nd December 1991.

(iii) Reply

IN THE HIGH COURT OF JUSTICE   **1991 E No. 5674**

QUEEN'S BENCH DIVISION

BETWEEN:

THE RIGHT HONOURABLE WALTER BARON ENRIGHT

<u>Plaintiff</u>

and

NELLIS AND SALMON (A Firm)   <u>Defendant</u>

REPLY

1. Save insofar as it contains admissions, the Plaintiff joins issue with the Defence.

2. It is denied that there was a warning notice at the top of the staircase at the time of the Plaintiff's fall, as alleged in Paragraph 2 of the Defence. Such a notice was put up only as the Plaintiff was being taken out of the said restaurant on a stretcher following his said fall.

Served the 14th day of January 1992 etc.

4. Trespass − declaration and injunction

(i) Statement of Claim

IN THE HIGH COURT OF JUSTICE   **CH 1991 F No. 8794**
CHANCERY DIVISION

(Writ issued the 5th day of June 1991)

BETWEEN: ANITA FOTHERING   <u>Plaintiff</u>
                                       and
                               NORMAN BROWNETT   <u>Defendant</u>

STATEMENT OF CLAIM

1. The Plaintiff is the freehold owner of the land and premises known as Westgate Farm, Haystacks Lane, Brokerville, Surrey, which is shown outlined in red on the plan annexed hereto.

2. The Defendant is the owner of the land and premises known as Fir Tree Cottage, Haystacks Lane, aforesaid, which is shown outlined in green on the said plan.

3. Since about the 15th November 1990, the Defendant and his servants have wrongfully entered and crossed the Plaintiff's said land, by crossing it along the line shown in blue on the said plan.

4. Further, in about January 1991, the Defendant's servants wrongfully constructed a wooden fence along either side of the said path.

5. By letter dated the 13th February 1991, the Plaintiff's Solicitors required the Defendant to cease to use the said path, and to remove the said fence or pay for its removal, but the Defendant has refused to do so, and has wrongfully claimed that the path is on his land.

6. Unless restrained by this Honourable Court, the Defendant is likely to continue to trespass onto the Plaintiff's said land.

7. By reason of the matters aforesaid, the Plaintiff has suffered loss and damage.

PARTICULARS

(a) Estimated cost of removing the said fence and disposing of it − £2,375;

(b) Estimated cost of re-turfing path worn by the Defendant's use − £1,500.

149

8. Further, the Plaintiff is entitled to and claims interest on such damages as he is awarded pursuant to Section 35A of the Supreme Court Act 1981 at such rate and for such period as this Honourable Court thinks fit.

AND the Plaintiff claims:

1. A declaration that the Defendant is not entitled to enter or cross the Plaintiff's said land along the line shown in blue or at all;

2. An injunction restraining the Defendant, by himself his servants or agents or otherwise howsoever from entering or crossing the Plaintiff's said land;

3. Damages;

4. Interest thereon under Paragraph 8 hereof to be assessed.

Served the 7th day of October 1991 etc.

(ii) Defence

IN THE HIGH COURT OF JUSTICE   **CH 1991 F No. 8794**

CHANCERY DIVISION

BETWEEN: ANITA FOTHERING   <u>Plaintiff</u>
and
NORMAN BROWNETT   <u>Defendant</u>

DEFENCE

1. Save that it is denied that the plan annexed to the Statement of Claim accurately shows the extent of the parties' land, Paragraphs 1 and 2 of the Statement of Claim is admitted. Annexed hereto is a plan showing the extent of the Plaintiff's land outlined in yellow, and the Defendant's land outlined in purple.

2. It is denied that the Defendant or his servants have ever entered or crossed the Plaintiff's land as alleged in Paragraph 3 of the Statement of Claim or at all. The blue line on the plan annexed to the Statement of Claim is entirely within the Defendant's land.

3. It is admitted that the Defendant has had constructed a fence alongside the path, but the path is entirely on his said land.

4. The Defendant admits receiving the letter referred to in Paragraph 5 of the Statement of Claim, but avers that his answer thereto was correct, namely that he owned the land over which the path runs and the fence.

5. Paragraphs 6, 7 and 8 of the Statement of Claim are denied.

6. In the premises, it is denied that the Plaintiff is entitled to the relief claimed or any relief.

Served the 11th day of November 1991 etc.

5. Assault and battery − personal injuries

(i) Particulars of Claim

IN THE BLOOMSBURY COUNTY COURT   **Case No. 9138475**

BETWEEN: LAWRENCE GREENEST   Plaintiff
                                         and
                            DEBORAH KINGPIN   Defendant

PARTICULARS OF CLAIM

1.   On the 30th June 1991, at about 12.30 p.m., the Plaintiff was walking along Hampleton Avenue, London SW20, when the Defendant assaulted and beat the Plaintiff by hitting him on the arm with a rubber hose pipe.

2.   By reason of the aforesaid, the Plaintiff suffered pain and injury.

PARTICULARS OF INJURY

Severe bruising of the upper left arm.

The Plaintiff was born on the 26th October 1958.

3.   Immediately after the said assault, the Defendant said to the Plaintiff, "If I ever see you in the area again, you'll get more of this". The Plaintiff fears that, unless restrained by this Honourable Court, the Defendant will continue to assault him.

4.   The Plaintiff is entitled to and claims interest on such damages as he is awarded pursuant to Section 69 of the County Courts Act 1984 at such rate and for such periods the Court thinks fit.

AND the Plaintiff claims:

1.   An order restraining the Defendant, by herself her servants or agents or otherwise howsoever from assaulting or beating the Plaintiff;

2.   Damages limited to £3,000;

3.   Interest under Paragraph 4 hereof, to be assessed.

Dated the 14th day of July 1991 etc.

Note

The claim for damages is worth less than £3,000. By limiting the claim to £3,000, if the Plaintiff loses, the costs he will have to pay will be limited to the new Scale 1.

(ii) Defence and Counterclaim

IN THE BLOOMSBURY COUNTY COURT   **Case No. 9138475**

BETWEEN: LAWRENCE GREENEST   <u>Plaintiff</u>
                              and
                        DEBORAH KINGPIN   <u>Defendant</u>

DEFENCE AND COUNTERCLAIM

DEFENCE

1. Save that it is admitted that at the time and place referred to the Defendant struck the Plaintiff with a rubber hose, Paragraph 1 of the Particulars of Claim is denied.

2. At about 12.25 p.m. on the said date, the Defendant was leaving her house at 65 Hampleton Road, aforesaid, when the Plaintiff leapt out from behind a bush in the Defendant's garden and grabbed the Defendant from behind, putting his arms around her throat. The Defendant called on the Plaintiff to stop, but he continued to strangle the Defendant, and acting in self defence, the Defendant grabbed a hose pipe and struck the Plaintiff, in order to make him release her.

3. No admissions are made as to the alleged injury.

4. Paragraph 3 of the Particulars of Claim is denied. The Defendant said to the Plaintiff: "If I ever see you outside my house again, I'll call the police".

5. In the premises, it is denied that the Plaintiff is entitled to the relief claimed or any relief.

6. Alternatively, if, which is denied, the Plaintiff is entitled to recover damages, the Defendant will seek to set off such sums as she is awarded under her Counterclaim herein, in extinction or diminution thereof.

COUNTERCLAIM

7. The Defendant repeats her Defence.

8. By reason of the Plaintiff's said assault, the Defendant has suffered injury, loss and damage.

PARTICULARS OF INJURY

Bruising to the neck and throat.

The Defendant was born on the 1st January 1959.

PARTICULARS OF SPECIAL DAMAGE

Cost of repairing damaged gold necklace — £125.

9. The Defendant fears that the Plaintiff will assault her and/or trespass in her garden or house unless restrained by the Court.

10. The Defendant is entitled to and claims interest on such damages as she is awarded pursuant to Section 69 of the County Courts Act 1984 at such rate and for such periods the Court thinks fit.

AND the Defendant counterclaims:

1. An order restraining the Plaintiff whether by himself his servants or agents or otherwise howsoever from

   (i) assaulting or beating the Defendant;
   (ii) entering or attempting to enter the Defendant's land or premises at 65 Hampleton Road, London SW20.

2. Damages;

3. Interest under Paragraph 10 hereof to be assessed.

Dated the 16th day of August 1991.

(iii) Reply and Defence to Counterclaim

IN THE BLOOMSBURY COUNTY COURT   **Case No. 9138475**

BETWEEN: LAWRENCE GREENEST   <u>Plaintiff</u>
and
DEBORAH KINGPIN   <u>Defendant</u>

REPLY AND DEFENCE TO COUNTERCLAIM

REPLY

1. Save insofar as it contains admissions, the Plaintiff joins issue with the Defence.

2. It is denied that the Plaintiff was ever in the Defendant's garden or assaulted her as alleged or at all.

DEFENCE TO COUNTERCLAIM

3. The injury, loss and damage alleged in Paragraph 8 of the Counterclaim is denied. Without prejudice to the generality of the denial, it is denied that the Defendant was wearing a necklace at the time of the incident.

4. It is denied that the Defendant is entitled to the relief counterclaimed or any relief.

Dated the 1st day of October 1991 etc.

154

6. Nuisance – smoke from neighbour – injunction and damages

(i) Particulars of Claim

IN THE STAINES COUNTY COURT   Case No. 9157297

BETWEEN:
     (1) WILLIAM FRENCH-FRY
     (2) MARGARET FRENCH-FRY   <u>Plaintiffs</u>
     and
     JONATHAN BUGGINS   <u>Defendant</u>

PARTICULARS OF CLAIM

1. The Plaintiffs are and were at all material times the freehold owners and occupiers of the premises known as 75 Greensleeves Lane, Staines, Middlesex. The Defendant is and was at all material times the owner and occupier of the neighbouring premises known as 77 Greensleeves Lane, aforesaid.

2. Since about the middle of February 1991, approximately every week, the Defendant has caused or permitted smoke, ash and pieces of burning rubbish from bonfires to spread from his premises onto the Plaintiff's premises.

3. The said smoke, ash and burning rubbish are a nuisance danger to the health of the Plaintiffs, their children and visitors. They have been and are continuing to suffer inconvenience and discomfort.

4. Further, the Plaintiffs have suffered loss and damage.

PARTICULARS OF SPECIAL DAMAGE

(i)   cost of replacing clothing on washing line burnt damaged by glowing particles of rubbish – £37.50.

(ii)   cost of erecting temporary fence – £150.

5. Unless restrained by this Honourable Court the Defendant will continue to create bonfires which cause the said nuisance.

6. Further, the Plaintiffs are entitled to and claim interest on such damages as they recover, pursuant to Section 69 of the County Courts Act 1984 at such rate and for such period as the Court shall think fit.

AND the Plaintiffs claim:

1. An order restraining the Defendant by himself his servants or agents or otherwise howsoever from continuing the said nuisance;

2. Damages limited to £5,000;

3. Interest under Paragraph 6 hereof to be assessed.

Dated the 23rd April 1991 etc.

(ii) Defence

IN THE STAINES COUNTY COURT   **Case No. 9157297**

BETWEEN: (1) WILLIAM FRENCH-FRY
                  (2) MARGARET FRENCH-FRY   Plaintiffs
                          and
                  JONATHAN BUGGINS   Defendant

DEFENCE

1. Save that it is denied that at all material times the Defendant was the occupier of 77 Greensleeves Lane, Paragraph 1 of the Particulars of Claim is admitted.

2. As to Paragraph 2 of the Particulars of Claim, from the 3rd January 1991 until the 18th April 1991, the Defendant was away from his said premises working in the United States. If, which is not admitted, smoke, ash or pieces of burning rubbish from bonfires went onto the Plaintiff's land, such bonfires were caused by squatters who unlawfully broke into and lived in the Defendant's premises while he was away, and over whom he had no control. The Defendant did not know of the presence of the said squatters until he returned from his said trip.

3. Paragraphs 3 and 4 of the Particulars of Claim are not admitted.

4. Paragraph 5 of the Particulars of Claim is denied. The Defendant has never lit a bonfire at his said premises, and has no intention of doing so in the future.

5. In the premises, it is denied that the Plaintiffs are entitled to the relief claimed or any relief.

Dated the 28th day of May 1991 etc.

7. Highways Act − breach of statutory duty to repair − personal injuries

(i) *Statement of Claim*

IN THE HIGH COURT OF JUSTICE   **1991 V No. 6879**

QUEEN'S BENCH DIVISION

SOUTHAMPTON DISTRICT REGISTRY

(Writ issued the 13th day of February 1991)

BETWEEN: MARIANNE VOLE   <u>Plaintiff</u>

and

SOUTH WALL COUNTY COUNCIL   <u>Defendant</u>

STATEMENT OF CLAIM

1. The Defendant is and was at all material times the highway authority in respect of the highway known as Pothole Lane, Begington, South Wall, Hampshire.

2. At about 11 a.m. on the 4th June 1990 the Plaintiff was riding her bicycle along the east pavement of the said highway, when the front wheel struck a ridge between 2 uneven paving stones, causing the said bicycle to crash into the wall alongside the said pavement.

3. The uneven paving stones, which were of a height difference of approximately 2½ inches, were the result of a breach of the Defendant's duty to repair the said highway under Section 41 of the Highways Act 1980.

4. By reason of the said accident, the Plaintiff suffered pain and injury, loss and damage.

PARTICULARS OF INJURY

(a) Fractured right ulna
(b) Severe bruising of the right knee and shin
(c) Shock.

The Plaintiff was born on the 5th August 1930.

PARTICULARS OF SPECIAL DAMAGE

Bicycle damaged beyond economical repair − cost of replacement − £325.

5.   Further, the Plaintiff is entitled to and claims interest on such damages as she is awarded pursuant to Section 35A of the Supreme Court Act 1981 at such rate and for such period as this Honourable Court thinks fit.

AND the Plaintive claims:
1.   Damages;

2.   Interest pursuant to Paragraph 5 hereof to be assessed.

Served the 22nd day of March 1991 etc.

(ii) Defence

IN THE HIGH COURT OF JUSTICE   **1991 V No. 6879**

QUEEN'S BENCH DIVISION

SOUTHAMPTON DISTRICT REGISTRY

BETWEEN: MARIANNE VOLE   <u>Plaintiff</u>
                                            and
                    SOUTH WALL COUNTY COUNCIL   <u>Defendant</u>

DEFENCE

1.   Paragraph 1 of the Statement of Claim is admitted.

2.   Paragraph 2 of the Statement of Claim is not admitted.

3.   No admission is made as to the alleged height difference. It is denied that the Defendant was in breach of its duty to repair or maintain the said highway. At all material times it took reasonable care to secure that the said highway was not dangerous for traffic, and the Defendant relies upon Section 58 of the said Act. The said highway was inspected approximately every 2 months, the last inspection before the Plaintiff's alleged accident having taken place on the 16th April 1990, when the said highway was found to be safe.

4.   Paragraph 4 of the Statement of Claim is not admitted.

5.   In the premises, it is denied that the Plaintiff is entitled to the relief claimed or any relief.

Served the 10th day of April 1991 etc.

8. Factories Act − breach of statutory duty − personal injuries

(i) Statement of Claim

IN THE HIGH COURT OF JUSTICE   1991 K No. 7888

QUEEN'S BENCH DIVISION

(Writ issued the 6th day of June 1991)

BETWEEN: GERALD BARRY KING   <u>Plaintiff</u>

and

CARBUNCLE PLC   <u>Defendant</u>

STATEMENT OF CLAIM

1.   At all material times, the Plaintiff was employed by the Defendant as a warehouseman at its premises Budgie Wharf, Linton Street, London EC1, to which the Factories Act 1961 applies.

2.   At about 11.30 a.m. on the 6th February 1989 the Plaintiff was walking down a spiral staircase at the North end of the said warehouse when he fell over a metal bucket which was on the said staircase, and fell down the stairs to the ground, which was slippery with a pool of water.

3.   The said accident was caused by the breach of statutory duty and/or negligence of the Defendant, its servants or agents.

PARTICULARS OF BREACH OF STATUTORY DUTY

(a)   In breach of Section 28(1) of the said Act, the stairs were not, so far as was reasonably practicable, kept free from obstruction.

(b)   In breach of the said Section 28(1), the floor was not, so far as was reasonably practicable, kept free from any substance likely to cause persons to slip.

(c)   In breach of Section 6 of the said Act, effective means were not provided and maintained for draining off the wet from the floor.

PARTICULARS OF NEGLIGENCE

(i)   The Plaintiff repeats the particulars of breach of statutory duty as allegations that the Defendant was in breach of its duty to provide the Plaintiff with a safe place of work.

    (ii)   The Defendant failed to warn the Plaintiff of the presence of the said bucket on the stairs.

4.   By reason of the aforesaid, the Plaintiff has suffered pain and injury, loss and damage.

PARTICULARS OF INJURY

(a)   Fracture of the left femur
(b)   Fracture of the left tibia
(c)   Severe sprain of the left ankle
(d)   Bruising to the chest.

The Plaintiff was born on the 2nd November 1947.

PARTICULARS OF SPECIAL DAMAGE

Loss of wages for 18 weeks from 6th February 1989 until the 12th June 1989 at £200 per week − £3,600.

Partial loss of wages for 3 weeks from 12th June 1989 until 4th July 1989 at £125 per week − £375.

Cost of replacing damaged trousers and shoes − £120.

5.   Further, the Plaintiff is entitled to and claims interest on such damages as he is awarded pursuant to Section 35A of the Supreme Court Act 1981 at such rate and for such period as this Honourable Court thinks fit.

    AND the Plaintiff claims:

1.   Damages;

2.   Interest thereon under Paragraph 5 to be assessed.

Served the 28th day of June 1991 etc.

(ii) Defence

IN THE HIGH COURT OF JUSTICE   **1991 K No. 7888**

QUEEN'S BENCH DIVISION

(Writ issued the 6th day of June 1991)

BETWEEN: GERALD BARRY KING   <u>Plaintiff</u>

                      and

            CARBUNCLE PLC   <u>Defendant</u>

DEFENCE

1.   Paragraph 1 of the Statement of Claim is admitted.

2. No admissions are made as to Paragraph 2 of the Statement of Claim.

3. It is denied that the Defendant, by its servants or agents was in breach of statutory duty or negligent as alleged in Paragraph 3 of the Statement of Claim or at all. The Defendant organised a system of regular inspection of all floors and staircases at the said premises to ensure that they were reasonably safe for employees to use, and such system satisfied the test of reasonable practicability.

4. It is denied that Section 6 of the Factories Act 1961 applies to the said premises, since no process is carried on which renders the floor liable to be wet to such an extent that the wet is capable of being removed by drainage.

5. Further or alternatively, the said accident was caused by the Plaintiff's negligence.

PARTICULARS OF NEGLIGENCE

(i)   Running rather than walking down the said staircase;
(ii) Failing to hold onto the bannister while descending the staircase;
(iii) Failing to look where he was going;
(iv) In the circumstances, failing to have sufficient regard for his own safety.

6. Paragraph 4 of the Statement of Claim is not admitted.

7. In the premises, it is denied that the Plaintiff is entitled to the relief claimed or any relief.

Served the 21st day of July 1991 etc.

(iii) Request for Further and Better Particulars of Defence

IN THE HIGH COURT OF JUSTICE   **1991 K No. 7888**

QUEEN'S BENCH DIVISION

BETWEEN: GERALD BARRY KING   Plaintiff
                                     and
                            CARBUNCLE PLC   Defendant

REQUEST FOR FURTHER AND BETTER PARTICULARS OF DEFENCE

Under Paragraph 3

Of "The Defendant organised a system of regular inspection of all floors and staircases at the said premises to ensure that they were reasonably safe for employees to use, and such system satisfied the test of reasonable practicability."

Request

(1) State how regularly it is alleged that the said staircase and floor were inspected.

(2) State who carried out the inspection.

(3) State the date and time the said inspection and floor were last inspected prior to 11.30 a.m. on the 6th February 1991.

Served the 31st day of July 1991 etc.

(iv) Further and Better Particulars of Defence

IN THE HIGH COURT OF JUSTICE   **1991 K No. 7888**

QUEEN'S BENCH DIVISION

BETWEEN: GERALD BARRY KING   Plaintiff
                                    and
                                    CARBUNCLE PLC   Defendant

**FURTHER AND BETTER PARTICULARS OF DEFENCE
PURSUANT TO REQUEST SERVED THE 31ST JULY 1991**

Under Paragraph 3

Of "The Defendant organised a system of regular inspection of all floors and staircases at the said premises to ensure that they were reasonably safe for employees to use, and such system satisfied the test of reasonable practicability."

Request

(1) State how regularly it is alleged that the said staircase and floor were inspected.

(2) State who carried out the inspection.

(3) State the date and time the said staircase and floor were last inspected prior to 11.30 a.m. on the 6th February 1989.

Reply

(1) Every weekday morning between 6 a.m. and 7 a.m.

(2) Fred Grimstock

(3) At about 6.30 a.m. on the 6th February 1989.

Served the 15th day of September 1991 etc.

9. Fatal accident – breach of statutory duty – Offices, Shops and Railway Premises Act

(i) Statement of Claim

IN THE HIGH COURT OF JUSTICE   1991 M No. 5563

QUEEN'S BENCH DIVISION

(Writ issued the 3rd day of October 1991)

BETWEEN: ELEANOR MORGAN
                      (Administratrix of the Estate of
                      HAROLD BOWEN deceased)   <u>Plaintiff</u>
                                              and
                      SAVERMEAT LIMITED   <u>Defendant</u>

STATEMENT OF CLAIM

1. The Plaintiff is the administratrix of the estate of Harold Bowen deceased, hereinafter called "the deceased", and brings this action for the benefit of his dependants under the Fatal Accidents Act 1976 and for the benefit of his estate under the Law Reform (Miscellaneous Provisions) Act 1934. Letters of Administration were granted to the Plaintiff out of the Principal Registry of the Family Division on the 14th June 1991.

2. At all material times the deceased was employed by the Defendant as a meat cutter at its premises known as Savermeat Supermarket, 132 Gore Lane, London SW3, which were shop premises within the meaning of the Offices, Shops and Railway Premises Act 1963.

3. On or about the 15th February 1991 was instructed by his supervisor to cut some beef on an electric meat slicer. As he was doing so his right arm came into contact with the blade and was severely cut.

4. The said accident was caused by the breach of statutory duty and/or negligence of the Defendant, its servants or agents.

PARTICULARS OF BREACH OF STATUTORY DUTY AND/OR NEGLIGENCE

(i) Negligently and/or in breach of Section 17(1) of the said 1963 Act, failing to fence the said blade, which was a dangerous part of the said machine, securely or at all.

(ii) Negligently and/or in breach of Section 19(1) of the said 1963 Act the deceased had not received sufficient training in work at the machine and/or was not under adequate supervision by a person having thorough knowledge and experience of the machine.

(iii) Negligently failing to provide the Plaintiff with a safe place or system of work.

5. By reason of the said negligence and/or breach of statutory duty, the deceased died subsequently on the 25th February 1991 by reason of the injuries that he had sustained, causing him pain and suffering, and his dependants and estate loss and damage.

PARTICULARS OF INJURY

(i) The Plaintiff's right arm was severely severed, and he suffered extreme pain and loss of blood, from which he later died. The Plaintiff was not fully sedated until approximately 3 hours after the accident, and was then in a coma until his death.

The Plaintiff was born on the 5th November 1953.

PARTICULARS PURSUANT TO STATUTE

(a) This action is brought on behalf of:

(i) The Plaintiff, a spinster, born on the 5th January 1957, who was living with the deceased in the same household immediately before the date of his death, and been so living with him for 6 years before that date and had been living during the whole of that period as the deceased's wife.

(ii) Patrick James Morgan, a child of the Plaintiff and the deceased, born on the 6th April 1983.

(b) The nature of the claim is that the deceased was a fit healthy man, aged 37, who had worked for the Defendant for 12 years. His take home pay was approximately £250 per week, of which he gave the Plaintiff approximately £150 per week for the support of herself and the said Patrick James Morgan. This would have continued had he lived.

(c) Funeral expenses paid by the Plaintiff – £760.

PARTICULARS OF SPECIAL DAMAGE

(i) Damage to deceased's clothing – £54
(ii) Damage to deceased's watch – £230.

6. Further, the Plaintiff is entitled to and claims interest on such damages as she is awarded pursuant to Section 35A of the Supreme Court Act 1981 at such rate and for such period as this Honourable Court thinks fit.

AND the Plaintiff claims:

1. Damages under the Fatal Accidents Act 1976 for the said dependants;

2. Damages under the Law Reform (Miscellaneous Provisions) Act 1934 for the benefit of the deceased's estate;

3. Interest under Paragraph 6 hereof to be assessed.

Served the 28th day of November 1991.

(ii) Defence

IN THE HIGH COURT OF JUSTICE   **1991 M No. 5563**

QUEEN'S BENCH DIVISION

(Writ issued the 3rd day of October 1991)

BETWEEN: ELEANOR MORGAN
                    (Administratrix of the Estate of
                    HAROLD BOWEN deceased)   Plaintiff
                                and
                    SAVERMEAT LIMITED   Defendant

DEFENCE

1. Paragraph 1 of the Statement of Claim is not admitted.

2. Paragraph 2 of the Statement of Claim is admitted.

3. Save that no admissions are made as to how the deceased's arm was cut, Paragraph 3 of the Statement of Claim is admitted.

4. Paragraph 4 of the Statement of Claim is denied. In particular, the deceased's supervisor Bert Vole had trained him for approximately 1½ hours in cleaning and using the said machine safely.

5. Further or alternatively, the said accident was caused wholly or in part by the deceased's negligence.

PARTICULARS OF NEGLIGENCE

(i)   In breach of express instructions, watching a pocket sized television, which he had placed on the counter next to the said machine, while cutting meat;

(ii)   Failing to look at the said machine whilst cutting meat on it.

(iii) Letting his arm come into contact with the blade of the said machine;

(iv)   Failing to have any or sufficient regard for his own safety.

6. It is denied that the said accident was caused by the negligence or breach of statutory duty of the Defendant. It is further denied that

165

the deceased would have continued to be employed by the Defendant had he lived. The Defendant would have dismissed him for watching television whilst working, having previously warned him not to do so. Save as aforesaid, Paragraph 5 of the Statement of Claim is not admitted.

7. In the premises, it is denied that the Plaintiff is entitled to the relief claimed or any relief.

Served the 14th day of December 1991 etc.

10. Sale of goods — misrepresentation and breach of contract

(i) Particulars of Claim

IN THE GUILDFORD COUNTY COURT   **Case No. 923456**

BETWEEN: SUZANNE SMITH   <u>Plaintiff</u>
                                           and
                    BANGERS GARAGES LIMITED   <u>Defendant</u>

PARTICULARS OF CLAIM

1. The Defendant is the proprietor of a second-hand car showroom at 54 Beechers Lane, Guildford, Surrey.

2. On the 16th July 1991, whilst the Plaintiff was looking at a Triumph Dolomite motor car registration no. TGH 768 W in the said showroom, one Jenkins, a servant of the Defendant, represented to the Plaintiff that the said motor car was in excellent condition, and had had 1 lady owner.

3. In reliance upon the said representation, the Plaintiff agreed to purchase the said motor car for £1,700.

4. There were express terms in the said agreement that the said motor car was in excellent condition and that it had had 1 previous lady owner only.

5. Further or alternatively, there were implied terms in the said agreement that the said motor car was of merchantable quality and fit for its purpose, namely being driven on roads.

6. The Plaintiff duly paid the Defendant the said price and took possession of the said motor car on the 17th July 1991.

7. The said representations were false and/or the Defendant was in breach of the said terms.

PARTICULARS

(i) The said motor car was not in excellent condition — it broke down 4 times within a period of 20 days after the 17th July 1991.

(ii) It required a completely new engine.

(iii) It had had 3 previous owners.

8. By reason of the said misrepresentation and/or breach of contract, the Plaintiff has suffered loss and damage.

167

PARTICULARS OF SPECIAL DAMAGE

Cost of supplying and fitting re-conditioned engine to the car — £950.

Bus and train fares while car broken down and/or being repaired — £47.50.

9. Further, the Plaintiff claims general damages for disappointment and inconvenience.

10. Further, the Plaintiff is entitled to and claims interest on such damages as she recovers, pursuant to Section 69 of the County Courts Act 1984, at such rate and for such period as the Court shall think fit.

AND the Plaintiff claims:

1. Damages limited to £3,000;

2. Interest under Paragraph 10 to be assessed.

Dated the 3rd day of January 1992 etc.

(ii) Defence

IN THE GUILDFORD COUNTY COURT   **Case No. 923456**

BETWEEN: SUZANNE SMITH   Plaintiff
                                        and
                          BANGERS GARAGES LIMITED   Defendant

DEFENCE

1. Paragraph 1 of the Particulars of Claim is admitted.

2. It is denied that the said Jenkins represented that the said motor car was in excellent condition. He said to the Plaintiff that it seemed to be all right for its age. Save as aforesaid, Paragraph 2 of the Particulars of Claim is admitted.

3. Save that no admission is made as to the alleged reliance, paragraph 3 of the Particulars of Claim is admitted.

4. Paragraph 4 of the Particulars of Claim is denied.

5. No admissions are made as to Paragraph 5 of the Particulars of Claim. The Plaintiff knew she was buying a fairly old second-hand car. Further, the said Jenkins asked whether the Plaintiff wanted it inspected by the Automobile Association before entering the said agreement, but the Plaintiff said No.

6. Paragraph 6 of the Particulars of Claim is admitted.

7. It is denied that the representations made by the said Jenkins were false or that the Defendant was in breach of contract, as alleged in Paragraph 7 of the Particulars of Claim or at all. As to the Particulars, the Defendant says:

    (i)   the Defendant makes no admissions as to the cause of the alleged breakdowns. The said Jenkins genuinely believed that the said car seemed all right for its age.
    (ii) No admission is made as to the allegation that the car required a new engine. The Defendant reserved the right to give further particulars, once the Plaintiff has provided facilities for the Defendant's engineer to inspect the old one.
    (iii) The car had only 1 lady owner. It had also had 2 male owners.

8. Paragraphs 8 and 9 of the Particulars of Claim are denied.

9. In the premises, it is denied that the Plaintiff is entitled to the relief claimed or any relief.

Dated the 5th day of February 1992 etc.

11. Repayment of loan — Limitation Act

(i) Statement of Claim

IN THE HIGH COURT OF JUSTICE   1991 D No. 8769

QUEEN'S BENCH DIVISION

(Writ issued the 1st February 1991)

BETWEEN: KENNETH LIONEL DAVIES   Plaintiff
                                    and
                                    ALI HUSSAR   Defendant

STATEMENT OF CLAIM

1. By an oral agreement made on the 4th November 1981, the Plaintiff loaned the Defendant the sum of £10,000 repayable on demand.

2. It was further agreed that, if the said sum was not repaid by the Defendant when demanded, he would pay to the Plaintiff interest @ 12% per annum from the date of demand until the date of repayment.

3. On the 1st August 1990, the Plaintiff demanded repayment of the said loan from the Defendant, but the Defendant has failed to pay the Plaintiff the said sum of £10,000 or any part thereof.

AND the Plaintiff claims:

1. The sum of £10,000;

2. Interest thereon @ 12% per annum from the 1st August 1990 until the date of issue of the Writ herein, amounting to £600, and continuing at the daily rate of £3.29 until judgment or sooner payment.

Served the 4th day of April 1991 etc.

(ii) Defence

IN THE HIGH COURT OF JUSTICE   1991 D No. 8769

QUEEN'S BENCH DIVISION

BETWEEN: KENNETH LIONEL DAVIES   <u>Plaintiff</u>
                              and
                   ALI HUSSAR   <u>Defendant</u>

DEFENCE

1.   Save that it is denied that the said loan was repayable on demand, Paragraph 1 of the Statement of Claim is admitted. The loan was repayable on the 4th November 1982.

2.   It is admitted that, if the said loan was not repaid on the 4th November 1982, interest was payable as alleged. Save as aforesaid, Paragraph 2 of the Statement of Claim is denied.

3.   Paragraph 3 of the Statement of Claim is admitted, but the Defendant relies upon Section 5 of the Limitation Act 1980 and contends that the Plaintiff's claim is statute barred, the cause of action having accrued more than 6 years before the issue of the Writ herein.

4.   In the premises, it is denied that the Plaintiff is entitled to the relief claimed or any relief.

Served the 30th day of April 1991 etc.

(iii) Reply

IN THE HIGH COURT OF JUSTICE   1991 D No. 8769

QUEEN'S BENCH DIVISION

BETWEEN: KENNETH LIONEL DAVIES   <u>Plaintiff</u>
                              and
                   ALI HUSSAR   <u>Defendant</u>

REPLY

1.   Save insofar as it contains admissions, the Plaintiff joins issue with the Defence.

171

2. If, which is denied, the loan was repayable on the 4th November 1982, it is denied that the claim herein is statute barred, since the debt was acknowledged by the Defendant on the 5th March 1987, when he wrote to the Plaintiff "I haven't forgotten about your money — be patient, I've been going through a bit of a rough patch recently." The Plaintiff will rely upon those words as an acknowledgement within the meaning of Sections 29(5) and 30 of the Limitation Act 1980. In the premises, the Plaintiff's right of action to recover the said sum accrued on and not before the 5th March 1987, namely within 6 years before this action was commenced.

Served the 14th May 1991 etc.

12. Sale of land − specific performance − misdescription

(i) Statement of Claim

IN THE HIGH COURT OF JUSTICE   CH 1991 H No. 9992

CHANCERY DIVISION

BETWEEN: HOWARD HOWLER   <u>Plaintiff</u>
                                      and
                               THEODORE THUMPETT   <u>Defendant</u>

STATEMENT OF CLAIM

1. By a written agreement dated the 14th March 1991 made between the Plaintiff and the Defendant, the Defendant agreed to purchase and the Plaintiff agreed to sell the freehold property known as "Dunpleading", Green Lane, Reading, Berkshire, at the price of £150,000.

2. There were express terms of the said agreement,
    (i)   that the Defendant would pay the Plaintiff by way of deposit the sum of £15,000, which sum was duly paid;
    (ii) completion of the sale would take place on the 16th April 1991.

3. In breach of the said agreement the Defendant failed to complete the said agreement on the 16th April 1991 and has since repeatedly refused to complete the said agreement.

4. The Plaintiff has at all material times and is now ready and willing to fulfil all his obligations under the said agreement.

5. The Plaintiff is entitled to and claims interest on such sums as he recovers pursuant to Section 35A of the Supreme Court Act 1981 at such rate and for such period as this Honourable Court thinks fit.

AND the Plaintiff claims:

1. Specific performance of the said agreement;

2. All necessary and consequential accounts and enquiries;

3. Damages for breach of contract in lieu of or in addition to specific performance;

4. Interest thereon under Paragraph 5 hereof;

5. A Declaration that the said deposit of £15,000 has been forfeited to the Plaintiff.

6.   Further or other relief.

Served the 28th day of May 1991 etc.

(ii) Defence and Counterclaim

IN THE HIGH COURT OF JUSTICE   CH 1991 H No. 9992

CHANCERY DIVISION

BETWEEN: HOWARD HOWLER   <u>Plaintiff</u>
                                    and
                           THEODORE THUMPETT   <u>Defendant</u>

DEFENCE AND COUNTERCLAIM

DEFENCE

1.   Paragraphs 1 and 2 of the Statement of Claim is admitted.

2.   The said agreement described, by way of a plan attached thereto, the property agreed to be sold as including a double garage.

3.   The said description was materially false in that the Plaintiff did not own the said double garage, and was and is unable to convey the same to the Defendant.

4.   In the premises, the Defendant is not obliged to complete the said agreement, and Paragraphs 3, 4 and 5 of the Statement of Claim are denied.

5.   It is denied that the Plaintiff is entitled to the relief claimed or any relief.

COUNTERCLAIM

6.   The Defendant repeats his Defence.

7.   By reason of the said misdescription, the Plaintiff is unable to convey to the Defendant the property as described in the said contract, but has wrongly refused to return the said deposit to the Defendant.

8.   The Defendant is entitled to interest on the said deposit under Section 35A of the Supreme Court Act 1981 @ 15% per annum from the 14th March 1991 until the date hereof, amounting to £562.50, and continuing at the daily rate of £6.16 until judgment or sooner payment.

AND the Defendant counterclaims:

174

1. The said deposit of £15,000;
2. Interest under paragraph 8 hereof amounting to £562.50 and continuing at the daily rate of £6.16 until judgment or sooner payment.

Served the 14th day of June 1991 etc.

(iii) Reply and Defence to Counterclaim

IN THE HIGH COURT OF JUSTICE   **CH 1991 H No. 9992**

CHANCERY DIVISION

BETWEEN: HOWARD HOWLER   <u>Plaintiff</u>
                                and
                    THEODORE THUMPETT   <u>Defendant</u>

REPLY AND DEFENCE TO COUNTERCLAIM

REPLY

1. Save insofar as it contains admissions, the Plaintiff joins issue with the Defence.
2. Paragraph 2 of the Defence is admitted.
3. Save that it is admitted that the Plaintiff did not own the said double garage, Paragraph 3 of the Defence is not admitted.
4. The said agreement incorporated the National Conditions of Sale (20th Edition), and the Plaintiff relies upon Condition 17, whereby no error, mis-statement or omission in the sale plan shall annul the sale, nor shall any damages be payable, or compensation allowed by either party in respect thereof.

DEFENCE TO COUNTERCLAIM

5. In the premises, it is denied that the Defendant is entitled to the return of the said deposit as claimed in the Counterclaim or at all.

Served the 5th day of July 1991 etc.

175

(iv) Rejoinder

IN THE HIGH COURT OF JUSTICE   CH 1991 H No. 9992
CHANCERY DIVISION

BETWEEN: HOWARD HOWLER   <u>Plaintiff</u>
                                              and
                                    THEODORE THUMPETT   <u>Defendant</u>

REJOINDER

Served pursuant to leave of Master Winkle dated the 20th July 1991

1.   The Defendant joins issue with the Plaintiff upon his Reply.

2.   As to Paragraph 4 of the Reply, Condition 17(1) is expressed to be subject to paragraph (2) (upon which the Defendant relies) which provides that paragraph (1) shall not apply to any error, misstatement or omission which is recklessly or fraudulently made, or any matter or thing by which the purchaser is prevented from getting substantially what he contracted to buy.

3.   Further or alternatively, in the circumstances of this case, the said term is not fair and reasonable within the meaning of the Unfair Contract Terms Act 1977.

Served the 12th day of August 1991 etc.

13. Landlord and tenant − possession − Rent Act − rent arrears and nuisance

(i) Particulars of Claim

IN THE WEST LONDON COUNTY COURT   Case No. **9148576**

BETWEEN: SLUMHOUSE ESTATES PLC   <u>Plaintiff</u>
                                                and
                                    M. R. BANKS (male)   <u>Defendant</u>

PARTICULARS OF CLAIM

1. The Plaintiff is the freehold owner and entitled to possession of the premises known as 54 Borneo Lane, London W14, hereinafter called "the premises", the rateable value whereof on the 31st March 1990 was £467.

2. By a tenancy agreement dated the 7th April 1973, Margaret Miller let the premises to Highfield Limited for a term of 5 years from the 25th March 1973 at a rent of £43 per month, payable on the first day of each month.

3. In or about May 1977, the residue of the said term was assigned to the Defendant.

4. After the expiry of the said term the Defendant became the statutory tenant of the premises within the meaning of the Rent Act 1977.

5. On the 6th September 1987, the reversion immediately expectant upon the determination of the said tenancy became vested in the Plaintiff.

6. From time to time the said rent has been increased in accordance with the said Act, and the registered rent since the 25th March 1990 has been £285 per month.

7. The Defendant is in arrears of rent, as follows:

   Balance of rent due 1st December 1990 − £130
   Rent due 1st January 1991   £285
   Rent due 1st February 1991   £285
   Rent due 1st March 1991   £285
   Total − £985

8. Further, the Defendant has been guilty of conduct which is a nuisance and annoyance to adjoining occupiers.

177

PARTICULARS

The Defendant plays music very loudly at night, waking the neighbours on either side of the premises. The neighbours have recently complained about the noise both to the Defendant and to the Plaintiff.

9. Possession of the premises is claimed pursuant to Case 1 and 2 of Schedule 15 to the said Act.

AND the Plaintiff claims:

1. Possession of the premises;

2. Arrears of rent of £985;

3. Rent/mesne profits @ £285 per month from the 1st April 1991 until possession is delivered up.

Dated the 25th March 1991 etc.

Note

As the rent is payable in advance, the rent due on the 1st March 1991 covers the position until the end of March.

(ii) Defence

IN THE WEST LONDON COUNTY COURT   **Case No. 9148576**

BETWEEN: SLUMHOUSE ESTATES PLC   <u>Plaintiff</u>
                                        and
                              M. R. BANKS (male)   <u>Defendant</u>

DEFENCE

1. Save that it is denied that the Plaintiff is entitled to possession of the premises, Paragraphs 1 to 6 of the Particulars of Claim are admitted.

2. As to paragraph 7 of the Particulars of Claim, on the 2nd December 1990, the Defendant gave to the Plaintiff's agent one Josiah Grabbe £155 rent and promised to pay the balance of £130 when he could afford it. On the 15th December 1990, he offered to pay the said Grabbe £75 towards the December rent, but was told to pay the whole amount or nothing at all. Thereafter, the Defendant became eligible to and applied for housing benefit in respect of his occupation of the premises. As a result of his application form having been lost by the housing benefit

authorities, he has not yet received any benefit. Once benefit is paid, the Defendant will be able to pay all the arrears. Accordingly, the Defendant contends that it would not be reasonable to make an order for possession under Case 1 of Schedule 15 to the Rent Act.

3. It is denied that the Defendant has made excessive noise so as to disturb his neighbours, as alleged or at all. On 1 occasion, the 14th January 1991, the Defendant held a party at the premises until 1 a.m. The neighbours asked him to turn the music down, which he did. Any complaints made to the Plaintiff were not genuine and motivated by the neighbours' anger at not being invited to the Defendant's party.

4. In the premises, it is denied that the Plaintiff is entitled to the relief claimed or any relief.

Dated the 8th day of April 1991 etc.

14. Landlord and tenant − possession − assured tenancy − breach of covenant

(i) Particulars of Claim

IN THE STOURBRIDGE COUNTY COURT   Case No. 91222365

BETWEEN: ENID NITPICKER   Plaintiff

and

HENRY LOUSE   Defendant

PARTICULARS OF CLAIM

1. By an agreement dated the 5th July 1990, the Plaintiff let the premises known as Flat 6, Boltwood Court, Huntingdon Road, Stourbridge, West Midlands, to the Defendant for 3 years from the 5th July 1990 at a rent of £340 per month, payable monthly in advance on the 5th day of each month.

2. The said agreement created an assured shorthold tenancy within the meaning of the Housing Act 1988, a notice in the prescribed form having been served by the Plaintiff's agent on the Defendant prior to the grant of the said tenancy, stating that the said tenancy was to be an assured shorthold tenancy.

3. By Clause 2(6) of the said agreement, the Defendant covenanted not to assign, sublet or part with possession of the said premises, or any part thereof without the prior written consent of the Plaintiff.

4. Clause 4(1) of the said agreement contained a proviso that the Plaintiff could re-enter the said premises, in the event of any breach of covenant by the Defendant.

5. In breach of Clause 2(6), the Defendant has sublet 2 rooms in the said premises without the Plaintiff's consent.

6. By a Notice in the prescribed form dated the 6th February 1991, and served on or about the 7th February 1991, the Plaintiff informed the Defendant of her intention to begin proceedings for possession not earlier than the 27th February 1991 and not later than 12 months from the date of service of the notice on the ground of breach of an obligation of the tenancy and specified the ground.

7. The Plaintiff claims possession of the said flat pursuant to Ground 12 of Schedule 2 to the said Act.

AND the Plaintiff claims:

1. Possession of the said flat;
2. Rent/mesne profits @ £340 per month from the 5th March 1991 until possession is delivered up.

Dated the 1st day of March 1991 etc.

(ii) Defence

IN THE STOURBRIDGE COUNTY COURT **Case No. 91222365**

BETWEEN:

ENID NITPICKER Plaintiff
and
HENRY LOUSE Defendant

DEFENCE

1. Paragraph 1 of the Particulars of Claim is admitted.
2. Paragraph 2 of the Particulars of Claim is denied. The Plaintiff's agent did not give the said Notice to the Defendant until about 1 hour after the said agreement was signed.
3. Paragraphs 3 and 4 of the Particulars of Claim are admitted.
4. Paragraph 5 of the Particulars of Claim is denied. The Defendant had a lodger staying in 2 rooms of the said premises for a period of approximately 5 months. It is denied that that amounted to a breach of covenant.
5. Save that service of the notice is admitted, Paragraph 6 of the Particulars of Claim is denied.
6. It is denied that the Plaintiff is entitled to possession as claimed or at all. If, which is denied, the Defendant was in breach of covenant, it would not be reasonable to make an order for possession, the lodger having left within 1 week of the service of these proceedings.
7. In the premises, it is denied that the Plaintiff is entitled to the relief claimed or any relief.

Dated the 23rd day of March 1991 etc.

(iii) *Request for Further and Better Particulars of Defence*

IN THE STOURBRIDGE COUNTY COURT   **Case No. 91222365**

BETWEEN: ENID NITPICKER   <u>Plaintiff</u>
                                        and
                                HENRY LOUSE   <u>Defendant</u>

REQUEST FOR FURTHER AND BETTER PARTICULARS OF THE DEFENCE

<u>Under Paragraph 4</u>

Of "The Defendant had a lodger staying in 2 rooms of the said premises for a period of approximately 5 months. It is denied that that amounted to a breach of covenant.

State

(1)   Whether the Defendant's agreement with the lodger was oral or written.

(2)   If oral, state all the terms agreed, including the amount of payment, whether the lodger had a key, who paid the bills and so on.

(3)   If written, state all the terms and supply a copy of the agreement to the Plaintiff's Solicitors.

Dated the 13th day of April 1991 etc.

(iv) *Further and Better Particulars of Defence*

IN THE STOURBRIDGE COUNTY COURT   **Case No. 91222365**

BETWEEN: ENID NITPICKER   <u>Plaintiff</u>
                                        and
                                HENRY LOUSE   <u>Defendant</u>

FURTHER AND BETTER PARTICULARS OF THE DEFENCE PURSUANT TO REQUEST DATED THE 13th APRIL 1991

<u>Request</u>

<u>Under Paragraph 4</u>

Of "The Defendant had a lodger staying in 2 rooms of the said premises for a period of approximately 5 months. It is denied that that amounted to a breach of covenant.

State

(1) Whether the Defendant's agreement with the lodger was oral or written;

(2) If oral, state all the terms agreed, including the amount of payment, whether the lodger had a key, who paid the bills and so on.

(3) If written, state all the terms and supply a copy of the agreement to the Plaintiff's Solicitors.

Reply

(1) Oral.

(2) The lodger paid the Defendant £35 per week for the use of the 2 rooms, plus one half of the electricity and telephone bills. He shared the bathroom with the Defendant. The Defendant gave him a key to the said flat. There were no locks on the doors of the 2 rooms occupied by the lodger.

Dated the 3rd day of May 1991 etc.

15. Landlord and tenant − forfeiture − breach of covenant to repair − damages

(i) Statement of Claim

IN THE HIGH COURT OF JUSTICE   CH 1991 P No. 6738

CHANCERY DIVISION

(Writ issued the 7th day of July 1991)

BETWEEN: PAYUP PROPERTIES PLC   <u>Plaintiff</u>
and
(1) TANNIC WINES LIMITED
(2) ALAN JEREMIAH GRAHAM   <u>Defendants</u>

STATEMENT OF CLAIM

1.   The Plaintiff is the freehold owner and entitled to possession of the premises known as and situate at 245 Waters Grove, London SE23, hereinafter called "the premises".

2.   By a lease made on the 27th May 1979, between Slumhouse Estates PLC of the first part, the First Defendant of the second part and the Second Defendant of the third part, the premises were let to the First Defendant for 21 years from the 25th March 1979, at a rent of £4,500 per annum, subject to review, payable quarterly in advance on the usual quarter days.

3.   By Clause 2(5) of the said lease, the First Defendant covenanted to keep the whole of the interior and exterior of the premises in good and substantial repair and condition throughout the said term.

4.   Clause 5 of the said lease contained a proviso for re-entry in the event, inter alia, of any breach of covenant by the lessee.

5.   By Clause 6(2) of the said lease, the Second Defendant covenanted as surety that the First Defendant would perform its covenants under the said lease, and that he would keep the lessor indemnified against any loss or expense occasioned by any breach of covenant by the First Defendant.

6.   Thereafter, the reversion immediately expectant upon the determination of the said term became vested in the Plaintiff.

7.   In breach of covenant, the First Defendant failed to keep the premises in good repair and condition, full particulars of the breaches being set out in a Schedule of Dilapidations attached to the Notice referred to in the next paragraph hereof.

8. By a Notice served by the Plaintiff's Solicitors on or about the 3rd March 1990, pursuant to Section 146 of the Law of Property Act 1925, the said breaches were specified, the First Defendant was required to remedy them within a reasonable time and to compensate the Plaintiff in money thereof.

9. The First Defendant failed to remedy the said breaches within a reasonable time or at all. On the 6th November 1990, Master Grockle in the High Court of Justice Queen's Bench Division, leave to commence forfeiture proceedings under the Leasehold Property (Repairs) Act 1938.

10. The First Defendant remains in possession of the premises, and the said lease has become forfeited to the Plaintiff.

11. By reason of the said breaches, the Plaintiff has suffered loss and damage.

PARTICULARS OF SPECIAL DAMAGE

Estimated cost of carrying out repair works − £55,000

Estimated loss of rental income for 4 months while work carried out £16,000.

12. No part of the premises comprises a dwelling-house.

13. Stronghold Bank Plc is the Defendant's mortgagee of the premises.

14. The value of the premises to the Plaintiff is £48,000 per annum.

15. The Plaintiff is entitled to and claims interest on such sums as it recovers pursuant to Section 35A of the Supreme Court Act 1981 at such rate and for such period as this Honourable Court thinks fit.

AND the Plaintiff claims:

Against the First Defendant

1. Possession of the premises;

2. Mesne profits @ £48,000 per annum, equivalent to a daily rate of £131.51, from the 29th September 1991 until possession is delivered up.

Against the Defendants and each of them

3. Damages for breach of covenant;

4. Interest under Paragraph 15 hereof, to be assessed.

Served the 2nd day of September 1991 etc.

(ii) Defence

IN THE HIGH COURT OF JUSTICE   CH 1991 P No. 6738

CHANCERY DIVISION

BETWEEN: PAYUP PROPERTIES PLC   <u>Plaintiff</u>
                                        and
                        (1) TANNIC WINES LIMITED
                        (2) ALAN JEREMIAH GRAHAM   <u>Defendants</u>

DEFENCE OF BOTH DEFENDANTS

1. Save that it is denied that the Plaintiff is entitled to possession of the premises, Paragraphs 1 to 6 of the Statement of Claim are admitted.

2. No admissions are made as to Paragraph 7 of the Statement of Claim.

3. Save that service of the Section 146 Notice is admitted, no admissions are made as to paragraph 8 of the Statement of Claim.

4. Save that the order of Master Grockle is admitted, no admissions are made as to Paragraph 9 of the Statement of Claim.

5. In December 1990 and January 1991, the First Defendant caused certain of the works to the roof of the premises, specified in the Section 146 Notice to be carried out. On the 1st February 1991, the Plaintiff's surveyor, Mr. Grout, approved the said works.

6. Thereafter, the Plaintiff accepted rent from the First Defendant, in respect of the March and June 1991 quarter days. By virtue of such acceptance of rent, the Plaintiff has waived the alleged breaches of covenant (which are not admitted), and is not entitled to forfeit the said lease.

7. Further or alternatively, it is denied that the Plaintiff has suffered the loss or damage alleged in Paragraph 11 of the Statement of Claim, or any damage. If, which is denied, the Plaintiff is entitled to recover possession of the premises, it intends to demolish the building presently standing on the site, and to build a new office block. The Plaintiff accordingly has suffered no diminution in the value of its reversion, and the Defendants rely upon the provisions of Section 18 of the Landlord and Tenant Act 1927.

8. Paragraphs 12 and 13 of the Statement of Claim are admitted.

9. Paragraph 14 of the Statement of Claim is denied.

10. It is denied that the Plaintiff is entitled to the relief claimed or any relief.

Served the 11th day of September 1991 etc.

Note

If no work specified in the s 146 notice has been done by a defendant, acceptance of rent will not waive a breach of repairing covenant, which is a continuing breach.

16. Interference with goods — purchase in market overt

(i) Statement of Claim

IN THE HIGH COURT OF JUSTICE   1991 H No.3345

QUEEN'S BENCH DIVISION

BETWEEN: HARVEY & BINGS (A Firm)   <u>Plaintiff</u>
                                            and
                                  J. R. HUNTER (female)   <u>Defendant</u>

STATEMENT OF CLAIM

1. The Plaintiff is and was at all material times the owner of a painting called "The Three Legged Horse" by Arnold Swindler, of the value of £20,000.

2. On or about the 15th November 1990, a person or persons unknown stole the said painting from the Plaintiff's premises at 654 Lincoln Street, Reading, Berkshire.

3. The Defendant is presently in possession of the said painting.

4. By a letter to the Defendant dated the 5th March 1991 the Plaintiff's Solicitors demanded the return of the said painting but the Defendant has wrongfully refused to return the same and still wrongfully detains the same.

5. By reason of the aforesaid, the Plaintiff has suffered loss and damage.

PARTICULARS OF SPECIAL DAMAGE

The Plaintiff had agreed to loan the said painting to the Wilon Gallery for 4 weeks from the 15th March 1991 at a fee of £300 per week, and has thereby lost the sum of £1,200.

6. Further, the Plaintiff is entitled to and claims interest on such damages as it is awarded pursuant to Section 35A of the Supreme Court Act 1981 at such rate and for such period as this Honourable Court thinks fit.

AND the Plaintiff claims:

1. The return of the said painting or £20,000 its value and damages; or

2. The return of the said painting and damages; or

3. Damages;

4.   Interest under Paragraph 6 to be assessed.

Served the 21st day of May 1991 etc.

(ii) Defence

IN THE HIGH COURT OF JUSTICE   **1991 H No. 3345**

QUEEN'S BENCH DIVISION

BETWEEN: HARVEY & BINGS (A Firm)   <u>Plaintiff</u>
                                           and
                                J. R. HUNTER (female)   <u>Defendant</u>

DEFENCE

1.   Save that it is denied that the Plaintiff is presently the owner of the said painting, Paragraphs 1 and 2 of the Statement of Claim are not admitted.

2.   Paragraph 3 of the Statement of Claim is admitted.

3.   The Defendant bought the said painting on or about the 26th January 1991 at Norrington Flea Market, which is a market overt. The Defendant purchased the said painting in good faith, according to the usage of the market and without notice of any defect in the title of the seller.

4.   It is admitted that the Plaintiff's Solicitors demanded the return of the said painting as alleged in Paragraph 4 of the Statement of Claim but denied that her refusal to return the same was wrongful. By reason of the aforesaid, she is entitled to keep the said painting.

5.   Paragraph 5 of the Statement of Claim is denied.

6.   In the premises, it is denied that the Plaintiff is entitled to the relief claimed or any relief.

Served the 15th day of June 1991 etc.

17. Dishonoured cheque — failure of consideration

(i) Statement of Claim

IN THE HIGH COURT OF JUSTICE   1991 V No. 6221

QUEEN'S BENCH DIVISION

(Writ issued the 18th day of June 1991)

BETWEEN: VILLAGE YOKELS (A Firm)   <u>Plaintiff</u>
                                                and
                                    J. N. WURZEL (Male)   <u>Defendant</u>

STATEMENT OF CLAIM

1. The Defendant drew a cheque for £10,000 dated the 5th May 1991 upon the Stronghold Bank PLC payable to the Plaintiff.

2. The Plaintiff duly presented the said cheque for payment on the 10th May 1991, but it was dishonoured, payment having been countermanded by the Defendant.

3. The Plaintiff claims interest under Section 57(1) of the Bills of Exchange Act 1882 @ 15% per annum.

PARTICULARS

Principal sum	£10,000.00
Interest at 15% per annum from	
10th May 1991 to date of Writ	160.27
	£10,160.27

AND the Plaintiff claims against the Defendant as drawer:

(1) The said sum of £10,160.27

(2) Interest pursuant to Section 57(1) of the said Act on the said sum of £10,000 @ 15% per annum, equivalent to a daily rate of £4.11 from the date of the Writ herein until judgment or sooner payment.

Served the 2nd day of July 1991 etc.

(ii) **Defence**

IN THE HIGH COURT OF JUSTICE   1991 V No. 6221

QUEEN'S BENCH DIVISION

BETWEEN: VILLAGE YOKELS (A Firm)   <u>Plaintiff</u>
                                and
                     J. N. WURZEL (Male)   <u>Defendant</u>

DEFENCE

1. Paragraph 1 of the Statement of Claim is admitted. The Defendant drew the said cheque in favour of the Plaintiff in consideration for the Plaintiff providing the Defendant with a timeshare agreement for a cottage in Bognor Regis, West Sussex.

2. It is admitted that, on the 8th May 1991, the Defendant countermanded payment of the said cheque. The Defendant discovered on the 7th May 1991 that the Plaintiff did not own any cottages in Bognor Regis, and that there was therefore no consideration for the said cheque.

3. In the premises, it is denied that the Plaintiff is entitled to the relief claimed or any relief.

Served the 16th day of July 1991 etc.

Index